The Great Monologues
from
The Women's Project

Smith and Kraus *Books For Actors*

THE MONOLOGUE SERIES
The Best Men's/Women's Stage Monologues of 1993
The Best Men's/Women's Stage Monologues of 1992
The Best Men's/Women's Stage Monologues of 1991
The Best Men's/Women's Stage Monologues of 1990
One Hundred Men's/Women's Stage Monologues from the 1980's
2 Minutes and Under: Character Monologues for Actors
Street Talk: Character Monologues for Actors
Uptown: Character Monologues for Actors
Monologues from Contemporary Literature: Volume I
Monologues from Classic Plays

FESTIVAL MONOLOGUE SERIES
The Great Monologues from the Humana Festival
The Great Monologues from the EST Marathon
The Great Monologues from the Mark Taper Forum

YOUNG ACTORS SERIES
Great Scenes and Monologues for Children
New Plays from A.C.T.'s Young Conservatory
Great Scenes for Young Actors from the Stage
Great Monologues for Young Actors
Multicultural Monologues for Young Actors
Multicultural Scenes for Young Actors

SCENE STUDY SERIES
Scenes From Classic Plays 468 B.C. to 1960 A.D.
The Best Stage Scenes of 1993
The Best Stage Scenes of 1992
The Best Stage Scenes for Women from the 1980's
The Best Stage Scenes for Men from the 1980's

CONTEMPORARY PLAYWRIGHTS
Romulus Linney: 17 Short Plays
Eric Overmyer: Collected Plays
Lanford Wilson: 21 Short Plays
William Mastrosimone: Collected Plays
Horton Foote: 4 New Plays
Terrence McNally: 15 Short Plays
Women Playwrights: The Best Plays of 1992
Humana Festival '93: The Complete Plays
Women Playwrights: The Best Plays of 1993

GREAT TRANSLATION FOR ACTORS SERIES
The Wood Demon: Anton Chekhov *translated by N. Saunders & F. Dwyer*
The Seagull: Anton Chekhov *translated by N. Saunders & F. Dwyer*
Three Sisters: Anton Chekhov *translated by Lanford Wilson*

OTHER BOOKS IN OUR COLLECTION
The Actor's Chekhov
Kiss and Tell: Restoration Scenes, Monologues, & History
Cold Readings: Some Do's and Don'ts for Actors at Auditions

If you require pre-publication information about upcoming Smith and Kraus monologue collections, scene collections, play anthologies, advanced acting books, and
books for young actors, you may receive our semi-annual catalogue, free of charge, by
sending your name and address to *Smith and Kraus Catalogue, P.O. Box 127 One
Main Street, Lyme, NH 03768 phone 1-800-862-5423, fax 1-603-795-4427.*

The Great Monologues from The Women's Project

edited by Kristin Graham

Festival Monologue Series

SK
A Smith and Kraus Book

Published by Smith and Kraus, Inc.
One Main Street, Lyme, NH 03768

First Edition: September 1994
10 9 8 7 6 5 4 3 2 1

NOTE: These monologues are intended to be used for audition and class study; permission is not required to use the material for those purposes. However, if there is a
paid performance of any of the monologues included in this book, please refer to
the permissions acknowledgment pages to locate the source who can grant permission for public performance.

Library of Congress Cataloging-in-Publication Data
Great monologues from the Women's Project / edited by Kristin Graham.
    --1st ed.
    p. cm. --(Monologue audition series)
    ISBN 1-880399-35-0 : $7.95

    1. Acting. 2. Monologues. 3. American drama--Women authors.
    4. American drama--20th century. 5. Women--United States--Drama.
    I. Graham, Kristin. II. Women's Project (New York, NY) III. Series.

PN2080.G722   1993
812'.045089287--dc20   93-30435
                                        CIP

Contents

Monologues for Women

Monologues For Men

Introduction

What kinds of roles do actors like to play? Those which reflect and illuminate the human condition; rich, complex characters who deal with the complications of life. What are women writing about? The human condition; rich, complex characters who are dealing with the complications of life. I am proud to introduce a collection of 50–some powerful monologues voiced by characters who range from pioneers to Vietnam Vets to Frida Kahlo. All written, of course, by women.

Like a peephole in a construction site, these monologues provide us with a window into the world that women are writing about. And it's a big world they're investigating; they're not dealing just with "women's issues", but life issues: racism, drug addiction, the breakup of a family, agoraphobia, marriage and relationship difficulties, etc. The characters grappling with these problems are from all backgrounds, time periods, and races. They are chained to a radiator in Harlem, or are lost in suburbia; they are world leaders or insurance salesmen. They are women and men who are making difficult choices, reaching important decisions, remembering the past, and observing life. Rich, complex characters dealing with life's mysteries...

It's also important that there are monologues for men in this collection. Women have been defined onstage by men from the Greeks onwards, so it's good to be able to turn the tables and see men through "the female gaze." How else to be able to ultimately get a balanced view of the universe if both male and female voices aren't heard?

30 women, 30 different windows on the world. 52 monologues, 52 rich characters—innumerable ways of playing them. These playwrights have given us wonderful, memorable roles, and now I share them with you.

—*Julia Miles*
Artistic Director, The Women's Project

The Great Monologues
from
The Women's Project

Women's Monologues

ACROBATICS
Joyce Aaron and Luna Tarlo

Set in a hotel room, *Acrobatics* is about two women, called simply "Woman" and "Girl," who spend their time talking about love and their liaisons with men. Their relationship to each other remains unclear.

Here, Girl, (20s), reads a letter she wrote to a Dutch boy she had a fling with.

GIRL: He's so thin. (*Pause.*) He sleeps a lot. Oh, he's probably crazy. Listen to this, I wrote him a letter. (*She goes to desk, takes out letter, gets back in bed, and reads.*) "Dearest love of mine, I am longing to be with you, close to you, to feel you, to touch you, to see you, to look at you, to want you, to talk to you, to laugh with you, to cry with you, to play with you, to fight with you, to desire with you, to wish with you, to dream with you, to listen to you, to watch with you, to hear with you, to rest with you, to eat with you, to awaken with you, to sleep with you, to seek with you, to find with you, to hunt with you, to wonder with you, to build with you, to destroy with you, to grow with you, to travel with you, to stand still with you, to be strong with you, to be weak with you, to remember with you, to forget with you, to mourn with you, to have joy with you, to be rich with you, to be poor with you, to be all with you, to make love with you, to wait with you, to rush with you, to swim with you, to drown with you, to float with you, to fly with you, to sing with you, to die with you, to live with you, to away with you, to reach with you, to burst with you, to more with you, and more with you, to be free with you, to be bound with you, to be me with you, to be you with you, to believe with you, to know nothing with you, to know everything with you, to run with you, to walk with you, to learn with you, to teach with you, to keep with you, to give away with you, to be pieces with you, to be whole with you, to be tired with you, to be an animal with you, to be a leaf with you, to be a tree with you, to be the grass with you, to be the sky with you, to be the dark with you, to be the light with you, to be the stars with you, to be the night with you, to be the day with you, to be the sun with you, to survive with you, to be the one with you, to be the many with you, to be God with you, to be nothing with you, to be everything with you, to be with you, to be with you . . ."

AFTER THE REVOLUTION
Nadja Tesich

After the Revolution is a drama about one family and America, in a hospital. As Michael lies unconscious, hit by a car, muttering about distant planets, various members of his family confront each other and their own dreams, lies, betrayals. They urge him to wake up.

Sitting next to her unconcious son, Rachel, (40s), an ex-dancer, talks about her marriage to Fred whom she had met in a hospital after her suicide attempt which she calls 'the flu'.

RACHEL: In the beginning, I was numb. It lasted a long time. Then, I cut my hair, it used to be very long, cut it short, much shorter than Michael's now.

They accepted me at a different school and I went. Everyone rejoiced how reasonable I had been about the whole thing. After all, you don't marry a struggling musician, and black at that.

I met Fred in a hospital when I was sick with the flu. He was in his last year of residency. He courted me with magazines and books on the hospital bed and when he proposed I didn't refuse.

Our wedding was traditional with parents, pictures, relatives, and dancing. Robert left for Europe in order to skip the event. He congratulated me with a postcard on my future middle-class life, doctor's wife and all.

His remarks didn't bother me at all. The marriage happened to someone else.

(*She turns suddenly to Michael.*) You were a miracle to me, you really were. Sure, you can laugh about "miracle." Thousands born every day and she calls it a miracle.

(*And then off.*) He was so perfect in every way that I even forgot he had something to do with my marriage. One day, he was still small, maybe about five, he asked me about the umbilical cord, if the doctors cut it with a knife or scissors and what would happen if you were in a jungle or a desert or a forest, who would do it then, especially if you had neither a knife or scissors. So, I said "I guess, if you had to, you could do it with your teeth, just like this." (*She demonstrates baring her teeth*.) My great-grandmother did it like that, or so we were told. He cringed, the poor thing. "It must hurt," he said. I wish I'd never said that; he seemed so scared.

On cold nights, with Fred at the hospital, we huddled together and fell asleep like two bears.

(*To him*.) Do you remember? "Once upon a time there were three bears. . . . The first one was very big, the second one less big, the third very tiny. . . . Talk to me please, just one word for me, please . . .

AFTER THE REVOLUTION
Nadja Tesich

After the Revolution is a drama about one family and America, in a hospital. As Michael lies unconscious, hit by a car, muttering about distant planets, various members of his family confront each other and their own dreams, lies, betrayals. They urge him to wake up.

Still alone in a hospital room, Rachel, (40s), talks about her marriage, her first love in back of her head.

RACHEL: On Sunday mornings, I would crawl out of bed and get a paper, the *Times* of course, and watch the young unmarried couples eating breakfast in the cafés around, that sleepy Sunday look in their eyes. I didn't really go in and stare at them, just passing by, sort of, stealing a glance through the window, never knowing really what they said to each other. It might have been quite ordinary, as a matter of fact, but from the outside, me on the street, them inside, they seemed so languorous and beautiful, and as they are always replaced by new young couples I never see them again. After that I would hurry home with the *Times*, eat ham and eggs with the family and do the puzzle and fight over who got more of what, and what to do in the afternoon.

Marriage kills, kills, kills, said somebody. Not true. Nobody got killed. Just a film over my face for those that do not know me. Me, Mrs. Cole, doctor's wife, mother of two, underneath still me. Cheers for me, still here! Once in a while, in the summer, all that heat and humidity brings back my body to me and I find myself moving, humming to the rhythm of the blasting radios of the young black boys as I walk to the store and back.

AFTER THE REVOLUTION
Nadja Tesich

After the Revolution is a drama about one family and America, in a hospital. As Michael lies unconscious, hit by a car, muttering about distant planets, various members of his family confront each other and their own dreams, lies, betrayals. They urge him to wake up.

Bonnie, a former girlfriend of Robert, Rachel's radical brother, observes the two of them (Robert and Rachel) through the glass at the hospital, as she remembers her breakup with Robert.

BONNIE: Maybe I'll come another time. My role is really a small one, not being one of the family. Robert and I talked a lot of marriage in the beginning and then he met Angela at a party his sister gave in his honor. She would have a lot of food and wine and music and we would come and stuff ourselves and marvel at the grown-ups at work. She was very clever, Rachel was. The women were always arranged in such a way that she, Rachel, appeared somehow bigger, smarter, handsomer than the rest of us in blue jeans. Maybe this is really unfair. She was more handsome and certainly more confident. It takes time to grow up and she had children and a husband even though we didn't see much of him. He was forever on call in some hospital. (*Laughter from RACHEL and ROBERT.*) And then Angela arrived. It was really an accident, you see. She was never invited, but since one of her friends, a young promising writer—it was that kind of a get-together, all budding poets, writers, activists of the Upper West Side getting together to exchange bagels and lox on Sundays, usually after a demonstration of some kind. Yeah. It was a Sunday in May and one of these guys invited Angela along. She was from somewhere in California and wrote major theoretical pieces for an avant garde journal that I never could read.

She was daring, all right. I have to give her credit for that, having always been timid myself. She wrote her name and phone number on a napkin and gave it to Robert while the rest of us stuffed ourselves on bagels.

(*This is said with admiration.*) I didn't see it happen, but I did see Robert's eyes, beautiful, dark, glowing, and knew something was up. He told me about it later, much later, when attempting to sing praises to her daring and lack of bourgeois norms, and how she never mentioned the word "marriage" to anyone, including him. This, you see, made her somehow superior and more worthy of . . . something. They stopped seeing each other a couple of summers ago, or more. I don't remember.

We stayed "in touch," as they say. Now we meet for coffee or a movie or things like that. Men need their mothers; I serve a function. Robert speaks of his loneliness, I about my work, and life goes on.

AMPHIBIANS
Molly Haskell

Russell and Pat Baring have invited their friends Emily and Lewis to dinner in their Manhattan apartment. Throughout the evening, cracks in both the friendships and the marriages are revealed.

Speaking to the audience, Pat reveals her obsession with Lewis.

PAT: Once I came to the beach not at noon but later, at dusk. I went around a rock where I couldn't be seen by anybody. I was finally going to take the plunge. I was having fantasies of Lewis. We'd had a strange . . . moment, the night before. Now, I felt as if Lewis were watching me, encouraging me, and I stripped, and walked as slowly as I could to the water, trying not to be self-conscious. There were very few people around, maybe I was afraid that God might be watching, taking notes. The water was the same temperature as the air. There was no shock or chill going in, nothing except undulating and weightlessness to mark the passage between one and the other. When I was finally immersed, I felt as if I were a part of it. Air, water and the surface of my skin were all one, and my body was no longer something that was beautiful or ugly, it just was. I never wanted to come back to land. I felt that if I came back I would have to become a human being, exchange my fins for two legs and not be able to move. But then I had this fantasy that I wasn't alone. I was with Lewis, and we had merged into some sort of sea creature, all slithery arms and legs, a new organism that could never exist on land.

Gravity was suspended, and so was responsibility. We were being washed into each other's arms, saying yes, no, yes, no, opening and closing like bivalves.

BLACK
Joyce Carol Oates

Debra O'Donnell, who is white, and her new lover Lew Claybrook, who is black, have invited her ex-husband, Jonathan Boyd, to dinner. Underneath a veneer of civility, the tensions between the three lead them into discussions of race, gender, and love.

Here, Debra remembers Boyd's domineering nature.

DEBRA: (*In a contemplative voice.*) Boyd always imagined he understood women. Not from the inside, of course—but from above.

"You don't want to do that, *really*"—he'd tell me. "You think so, but *really* you don't." (*Pause.*) "You don't like those people." "You do like these people"—*his* friends. (*Laughs.*) Once, I was a kid, thirteen years old, there was a traveling carnival near one of the Army bases where my father was stationed, everyone from the base went, and one of the acts was a hypnotist . . . a man probably not that old but he had a beard, pearly-gray hair, wore a tux . . . he invited "subjects" up on stage, and my girl friends pushed me up, and . . . (*Debra has been moving about, conscious of the men's eyes on her.*) . . . God, why am I telling this! I'm drunk. (*Laughs.*)

[**BOYD/CLAYBROOK**: (*Not quite in unison.*) Go on, don't stop.]

DEBRA: Up there on the stage, I was so scared I thought I'd faint! All those people in the audience . . . looking at me! The hypnotist called himself "Dr. Night" and he told me he was going to "subvert my will" and it would be "painless" and demonstrate the "higher powers of the intellect." He waved his fingers in front of my eyes and said in this deep gravelly voice, "When I count to ten you will be a little girl again, five years old," and he started in counting, and everything began to swim around me, I could feel my . . . consciousness . . . get smaller and smaller like a candle flame about to go out, he gets to "eight, nine, ten," and wiggles his fingers in some kind of hocus pocus, but I was still awake, I saw he was wearing pancake makeup and I could smell whiskey on his breath, I knew I wasn't doing it right, I wasn't hypnotized like I was supposed to be, and he saw it, too, he was sweating and angry and did it over again, "When I count to ten you will be a little girl, five years old," so the poor guy tries it again, and again I'm . . . (*Pause, laughs.*) . . . in my own mind. (*Pause.*) I couldn't be hypnotized.

BREAKING THE PRAIRIE WOLF CODE
Lavonne Mueller

This play deals with the hardships a mother and daughter face on a wagon train, heading West.

Bluster, one of the officers on the wagon train, chatters incessantly to Helen as he digs a grave for her dying fourteen-year-old daughter. When Helen can endure no more of Bluster, Esther, an older black woman on the train, takes over the painful job of digging while dispensing both wisdom and comfort to the distraught mother.

ESTHER: "I could a tale unfold whose lightest word would harrow up the soul." (*Pause.*) Hamlet Shakespeare.

[**HELEN:** I'm trying to be brave.]

ESTHER: What can't be cured must be endured.

[**HELEN:** How did you stand it?]

ESTHER: I rocked . . . outside on the porch. So folks could see me. When you're moving, it's cool. And it's stately. Sitting is a pastime for notables in Africa. Hundreds of people watch you sit . . . in Africa. (*ESTHER goes to HELEN and takes the shovel from HELEN. ESTHER talks as she digs.*) I'd give you my old rocker, but I can't stand to part with it. I used it on all my children . . . tapping with one foot and kicking the rocker with the other. My husband says I carry too much junk. But I always tell him: "William Bibbs, junk don't eat nothing. Long as it don't eat, I keep it." (*ESTHER stops digging. She takes a handerchief out of her pocket.*) This belonged to my child, Alice. It's the only nice cloth I got that don't be flour sacking. (*Pause.*) Take it. (*HELEN takes the handerkerchief.*)

(*As she digs.*) We was headers together. We carried cotton on our heads. (*Pause.*) My Alice wore this handkerchief under all the cotton . . . to keep her pretty hair nice. (*Pause.*) We walked all day in the sun. Our heads hurt. Our brains hurt. My Alice, she be only twelve and we had to keep walking 'cause by the end of the day, we had to carry hundreds of bags of cotton to the Plantation shed. (*Pause.*) Sometimes my Alice . . . she'd stop . . . and fan her little breasts like the flutter of a mountain bird. Just watching her cooled me. And I'd say: Alice, someday, we'll go out West.

[HELEN: I want to be strong like you, Esther. But it's hard. It's . . . so hard.]

ESTHER: Sometimes, the mornings be so nice . . . a breeze floating gentle with the spicy smell of pimento trees. I walking beside my little girl . . . watching her tiny feet so dainty going past all them rows of pickers. (*Pause.*) Alice is married now. With children of her own in Arkansas. I probably won't never see her. I'm in the West now.

[HELEN: Tell me what to do, Esther.]

ESTHER: We have a saying in Africa. "Talking with one another is loving one another." You remember that. (*Pause.*) Put the handkerchief over your child's face—in the end.

(*Pause.*) Hard as those cotton days was . . . I pine to walk beside my daughter all day long.

CHAIN
Pearl Cleage

Rosa, a sixteen-year-old black girl addicted to crack, is chained by her desperate but misguided parents to the radiator of their small apartment.

Rosa explains why Jesus started using crack.

ROSA: Jesus mama had a boyfriend, right? And the nigga was a crackhead and she hid his shit from him. Call herself tryin' to help him get off it. Well, she wouldn't tell him where the shit was, so he shot her right there in their apartment, went through all her shit until he found it, and was sittin' there smokin' it when Jesus came home. Jesus mama layin' right on the floor in the next room, dead as shit, and this nigga so high he don't even give a fuck. Jesus say the nigga didn't even tell him she was dead. He just looked up when he walked in and said, *"Your mama in the kitchen."* When he came back out, the nigga was gone. (*A beat.*) I told you it was some terrible shit.

So after they buried her and shit, Jesus said he started thinkin' about that nigga just sittin' there smokin' while his mama layin' in the next room dead and he said he just thought, well, fuck it. *If the shit that damn good, let me have it.* I told him he was just thinkin' that way 'cause he felt bad about his mom and shit, but he said he wadn't askin' me if he *should* do it. He was just tellin' me.

He didn't act like no addict either. He don't act like one now, unless he can't get the shit, then he start actin' weird. Talkin' crazy and shit. When Jesus need to get high, he talk about killin' people a lot. He ain't never killed nobody, but he talk about that shit a lot when he can't get high. I know it's because of his mama, so I try to change the subject so he won't go off on it. Paula be scared of Jesus when he talk that shit, but she ain't know him as long as I have. I been knowin' Jesus since I was eleven years old. How he gonna scare me after all that?

13

CHAIN
Pearl Cleage

Rosa, a sixteen-year-old black girl addicted to crack, is chained by her desperate but misguided parents to the radiator of their small apartment.

After being chained for 5 days, Rosa begins to think about her addiction and consider its consequences.

Rosa: I been thinkin' 'bout if I wanna keep smokin' that shit or not. No, I mean really thinkin' about it for myself. It can make you do shit that is really fucked up. I done some fucked up shit myself when I was high, or tryin' to get high. I told you I stole my grandmamma's check. I stole lots of people checks. Cash and carry. Old people be lookin' all worried 'cause they check ain't come and I know I smoked that shit up two days ago. And you don't care neither! You just say, *fuck it.*

Like, I keep thinkin' 'bout how Jesus left me with them niggas I didn't even know! He didn't care what they did to me. They coulda thrown me out the window...*And they do that shit, too!* Old crackhead niggas threw a girl out the window right around the corner from here just a week ago. Took her clothes off first so when she hit the ground her titties and shit was all out. People standin' around laughin' and she dead as shit. Nobody even covered her up or nothin'.

My daddy told me only God stronger than crack. I tell him this chain been doin' a pretty good job. I was just kiddin', but I think it made him feel bad 'cause his face got all sad and shit. (*A beat.*) I told him I just meant it's hard once you can come and go when you want to not to just go anywhere you can think of goin', right? Even if you not thinkin' about it by yourself, somebody gonna remind me to think about smokin' that rock. They gonna be goin' there, or comin' from there or lookin' for some money to get there or *somethin'*. It's not like you gotta be lookin' for the shit. (*A beat.*) He told me he knew I was a good girl and he trusted me. I wanted to say, *hey, man!*

This is goddamn Harlem! Trust ain't in it! (A beat.) I don't trust nobody. *(A beat.)* Not about no shit like this. It ain't a goddamn thing out there but a bunch of niggas gonna die and wanna take me wid 'em. *Ain't a thing out there. (She looks around.)* At least in here, ain't nobody fuckin' with me. I got food. I got a bathroom. I even got TV and shit, so how bad can it be? *(Suddenly angry.) And what the fuck you lookin' at?*

CHOICES

conceived by Patricia Bosworth,
adapted by Cay Michael Patten and Lily Lodge

Choices is a collection of quotes and writings by various women of renown who have all had to make difficult choices in life.

Playwright Patricia Bosworth describes the summer she pretended she was a boy.

PATRICIA BOSWORTH: I remember the summer I was ten and I was told at the Country Club Pool that I could no longer dive off the high diving board. "Girls don't do that. Only boys can," the lifeguard said. Well that made me furious, because I'd been diving off the high diving board all summer just beautifully. I loved diving off that board. I loved the rush of excitement, the sense of danger.

Anyhow, I decided then and there it would be better for my career at least to become a boy. I cut off my hair and I dressed as a boy and I gave myself the name of Bill. I was so determined to play out this new role, that I refused to go into the ladies room to change into my bathing suit. I wasn't allowed into the men's room so I changed outside, very quickly. I can now change very quickly anywhere.

Throughout that entire summer as Bill, I swam, played tennis, rode horseback better than any of the boys I knew. One boy, Charlie, became a particular friend of mine. Then he got rheumatic fever and had to stay in bed. I visited him and read him stories, and we would occasionally talk man to man.

By September Charlie was well again, and his mother phoned my mother to say she was giving Charlie a swimming party for all the little boys, a skinny dip party, and she wanted Bill very much to come.

As soon as my mother hung up the phone she ran to me and said "What are we going to do Bill? We're going to have to tell them." So it came out I was a girl. It was the end of summer and the end of Bill.

My mother was wonderful about the whole thing. She acted as if everything I'd done as Bill was perfectly all right with her. I've never forgotten that.

COLETTE IN LOVE
Lavonne Mueller

Colette In Love explores the famous French author's need to write and to love and the conflict between those two needs.

Colette has just rejected her old lover and mentor, Willy. She is tired of 'ghost writing' his novels. This scene follows immediately after a quarrel in which Willy, as he is leaving, predicts her failure without him.

COLETTE: I've never been able to cry with ease, decency and fitting emotion. (*Pause.*) I detest tears. They're too hard for me to conquer.

(*COLETTE begins to put mascara on her eyelashes and speaks to Lola the bird.*)

One thing that keeps me from crying, Lola, is putting mascara on my eyelashes. (*She stops with mascara and studies herself in the mirror.*) The corners of my mouth where I smile have already started to engrave a sad line. And round my throat, that triple necklace of Venus is pressed a little more deeply into my flesh every day by an invisible hand. (*Pause.*) Is that a writer in there? What if . . . I can't write by myself? What if . . . they were Willy's words, after all. What if nothing were left of me but a streak of dyed color stuck to the mirror like a long muddy tear. (*Pause. To bird.*) Lola, are we really vagabonds? (*Pause.*) I'm beginning to talk to myself. Holding conversations with my bird . . . and the fire . . . and my own reflection. It's a habit recluses and old prisoners fall into. But I'm not like them. I'm free.

EATING CHICKEN FEET
Kitty Chen

Teenage Chinese-American Betty Sung's parents hadn't spoken in over five years when she walked in front of a car in a desperate attempt to bring them together. As they gather around her hospital bed, the family is finally forced to reveal their problems.

Here, Betty rises from her coma to address the audience.

BETTY: One day, five years ago, the end of the world came. I sat on the grass and watched the moving men load the truck. All the furniture was on the lawn, the dining room set, the cherrywood dresser, sofas, mattresses. All her bags and trunks, and boxes and boxes and boxes. Furniture always looks so sad outside of a house. Have you noticed that? Awkward. Sort of naked . . . mentally ill. Legs in the air at crazy angles, white bellies showing. It's funny how you see all the dents and gouges and chipped paint you never saw before. Everything looked so shabby. For a moment I was almost happy to see it go. Then suddenly I had this fear, I *knew*, that they were going to pull up my house and put it in the truck. It hit me like a twig thwacks back in your face. Everything would be gone. There'd be nothing left but an empty lot full of weeds. (*Jumps up.*) "Put it back! Put it back! You can't take my house!" But they don't hear me. I hit them and punch them in the face, but they don't notice. "Mom! Dad! Make them stop! Make them bring my house back!" But they're just standing there . . . looking at the air and not seeing anything. "Do something! Do something before it's too late!" They keep looking at the air. I'm screaming but no one hears me, nobody does anything. What am I going to do? STOP IT! STOP IT! (*Suddenly covers her eyes with her hands.*) If I close my eyes . . . and *wish real hard* . . . everything will be all right. Any minute now she's going to say, "Open your eyes. No one's leaving, no one's taking the house. I've just been fooling you. This is just a joke, a test. Just want to see if you're a good girl." When I open them, my house will be back in the ground. The furniture will zip back in like a movie playing backwards. The piano will be in its place under the staircase. The dining room table will be all set for dinner. . . . Everything will be the way it's supposed to be. . . . And I will have a happy family.

ENTRY POINTS
Sharon Houck Ross

A southern family comes together and remembers their shared past when Mamaw, the mother and grandmother who raised them, is dying.

Summer, a recent divorcée in her thirties, describes a visit with her son, who lives with his father.

SUMMER: Five, four, three, two, one and one half, one, zero. Okay Jeremy, come on out of the closet. We have to eat supper before it's time for you to go back to Dad. Your jello brontosaurus is going to melt before you even get to see him jiggle. He's lime green with orange carrot shreds for hair. (*Pause.*) Maybe you just need a hug, is that it? I haven't had a good hug today, either. I'm crawling in there with a big He-Man hug and a She-Ra kiss. Ready or not, here I come.

(SUMMER *tries to open the door.*)

Okay. Will you at least tell me why you're mad? We were having fun playing Fireball Island. Did I say something? What did I do? (*Pause.*) Here, I tell you what. I'm sliding paper and a crayon under the door. You draw a picture or write a note for me, okay? Jeremy, I'm still your mommy. It doesn't matter where I live. I'll always be your mommy.

(*Paper slides out. She reads it.*)

You want to go home to Dad. But this is *our* time. I get to see you only one night a week and I miss you. I miss you a lot.

(*Another sheet comes out; she reads it and tries not to cry.*)

I know you do. But I don't hate *you*. I love you. You're my little boy-who-can-do-anything, remember? (*Listening.*) Honey, are you crying? Come on out and let me hold you. Please.

(*Silence. She gets the hamster cage.*)

ENTRY POINTS
Sharon Houck Ross

A southern family comes together and remembers their shared past when Mamaw, the mother and grandmother who raised them, is dying.

From her hospital bed, Mamaw imagines telling her own mother about her new love.

MAMAW: (*Picking peas.*) Remember, Mama? You taught me how to play the piana with that old song. And I taught each one of my girls. You found your hero, didn't you? When I first married, I thought Buck was going to be mine. But then all the children came along. Funny how two people under the same roof can be living on separate planets. You told me he'd come around, like Papa did for you. You told me I just had to make myself wait long enough, remember? I kept on waiting, Mama. Like you told me. I was waiting right up to the minute he died. (*Pause; carefully announcing.*) And now, Mama, now there's Jonathan, my sweet Jonathan. He's joining us for dinner to-night. Just meet him. Here, at least look at his picture—isn't he—

   (*MAMAW sees MAMA exit.*)
   I am not a married woman, Mama—Buck's dead!

FOUR CORNERS
Gina Wendkos and Donna Bond

Four Corners explores the life of a middle-aged woman who is an acute agoraphobic, someone who is terrified to leave her house, and the resulting emotional distress on her teenage son and husband.

Anna, who hasn't left her house in ten years, describes why she refuses to go out.

ANNA: Oh, I have many opinions. Yes, I indeed have many opinions. But I am not one of those types of people who feel they have to be everywhere, do everything, see everyone. Nope. Not me. I'm secure with myself. I know myself. Do *you? Do you?* Well, I do. And I don't mind telling you what I know. I know what I like. I like television. I like my own company. I do *not* like the chatter of others. I like my house. I *love* my house. I'm not ashamed of loving the simple things in life. I do not need a circus. I do not need a parade. I need my things. The things that matter to *me.* And who are you to judge what matters to me, huh? I don't judge you. . . . No, I *don't.* Do I judge you for wanting to traipse all over town pretending you're happy? Drive here, drive there, act like a big shot! You're no big shot, missy, no you are not! You think you're big stuff because you go *shopping?* I could do that! Why should I want to? You think you're talented because you go to the beauty parlor? *Who can't?* I *choose* not to, do you hear me? I choose not to! And when I choose to . . . do you hear me? . . . When I choose to, I will!

And that's quite simply the whole story. When I damn well feel like doing anything I damn well want, you can bet I damn well will! And stop acting like you're so important, because you're nothing but a piece of shit, sitting there like you're ever so smart and fancy. . . . Well, I don't mean really that you're a piece of shit, exactly. I mean maybe you don't understand. You see, I'm not just different; I'm *special.* You would be special too if you made your own life, your own world, your own *air*. I make my own air. I don't breathe other people's air. I breathe my own. And what's in these four corners is my own air.

FOUR CORNERS
Gina Wendkos and Donna Bond

Four Corners explores the life of a middle-aged woman who is an acute agoraphobic, someone who is terrified to leave her house, and the resulting emotional distress on her teenage son and husband.

Fantasizing, Anna speaks on the phone as though someone were listening to her.

ANNA: OH, HI, HOW TERRIFIC TO HEAR FROM YOU. It's been months! How's SAM? The kids? GREAT! THAT'S REALLY TERRIFIC TO HEAR! OH, THEY'RE FINE. . . . OH, I'll tell them, certainly. . . . Really? Yes, I've seen them. . . . they're terrific. . . . yes, I know . . . and I LOVE THE LUNCHES THERE TOO . . . OH, I do, all the time. . . . (*Giggles.*) . . . the shrimp salad. . . . it's scrumptious! (*Giggles.*) WELL, then of course, a game of tennis. . . . then you don't feel quite so bad. . . . I mean about the salad, it's not that fattening. . . . but still, all that mayonnaise. . . . (*Giggles.*) . . . RIGHT WHERE I don't need it. haha
(This is treated in a hyper chatter—almost manic.)
Can we visit this evening? Oh, I know RALPH would love to . . . I'll make my sponge cake and I'LL PUT ON THAT LEMON FROSTING. . . . you still like that, don't you. . . . I still make it good. *OH YES I DO!* (*Repressed anger.*) WELL, any ol' way, I'll do it . . . and you'll like it. Oh yes, you will . . . because when I shape them, my brownies, like little stars. . . . I AM THE BELLE OF THE BALL. THE STAR OF THE NIGHT! AND THERE IS NO MISTAKE ABOUT THAT. AND I WILL MAKE THEM WHEN I WANT TO! I LIKE BEING THE TALK OF THE TOWN. AND I AM WHEN I MAKE MY STAR SHAPED BROWNIES. I like being excellent at what I do. And why not? People laugh at you if you're a failure . . . and that's not going to happen to me . . . on no sireeee. You think people are kind, well . . . let me remind you, they are not kind. THEY ARE HIDEOUS. THAT'S right! I said hideous and I don't just mean hideous. . . . I MEAN

VILE. Not that I've ever failed . . . *oh, no I haven't*. BUT, BUT . . . I've seen failures and also I've seen what people do to failures. They don't let you forget oh, no they don't. THEY TELL THE WORLD. THEY EMBARRASS YOU. HA! CAN YOU IMAGINE THE CRUELTY OF PEOPLE, AS IF failure weren't enough for the poor soul, on top of that THEY EMBARRASS YOU. (*Giggles.*) I mean, not that I know, of course, but I've seen what happens to failures, oh yes, I have . . . and it is not a pretty sight.

FRIDA: THE STORY OF FRIDA KAHLO
book by Hilary Blecher
monologues and lyrics byMigdalia Cruz

Produced by the American Music Theater Festival with contributions from the Women's Project and Productions and the Houston Grand Opera. This musical play is based on the relationship of Frida Kahlo, one of the twentieth century's important surrealistic painters, with renowned painter/muralist Diego Rivera.

While her husband paints a mural for the RCA building in New York, Frida is interviewed by a reporter.

FRIDA: Yes, I'm also an artist . . . but, not like Diego. Little things . . . nothing serious. . . . No, I didn't study with him or anyone else. One day, I just started to paint. . . . He paints the big-outside, and I paint the secrets inside. . . . It makes for a very pretty marriage. Oh . . .

(*She leans forward and whispers mischievously.*)

And there's only one thing Diego likes to do almost as much as paint . . .

(*Laughs.*)

Make love . . . especially to me.

No, it doesn't hurt. But I understand the question . . . me, with my uterus pierced by a handrail—like a sword through a bull. I'm small, but I have tough skin—It's the German in me, I think. Or maybe the Jew. I know how to fight and what to fight for. Love, sex, cigarettes and tequila. Not Painting . . . that's just a fact, like taking a breath on a cold day—you see it going out before it has a chance to go down—proving you're alive. . . . Self-portraits? Well, why not look out and see yourself as others see you? I prefer to suffer in a Catholic way—publicly. And I never complain . . . well, almost never. I simply paint . . . and I want this baby.

FRIDA: THE STORY OF FRIDA KAHLO
book by Hilary Blecher
monologues and lyrics byMigdalia Cruz

Produced by the American Music Theater Festival with contributions from the Women's Project and Productions and the Houston Grand Opera. This musical play is based on the relationship of Frida Kahlo, one of the twentieth century's important surrealistic painters, with renowned painter/muralist Diego Rivera.

After selling a painting to the Louvre in Paris, Frida, back in New York, has a voluptuous conversation with her lover, Nickolas Muray, a famous photographer.

FRIDA: I'm so happy to be back in our New York, Nick. . . . I hated Paris so much. Everything here reminds me of you now. The "Half Moon" at Coney Island is your lips and every tree in Central Park shades only us from the sun. I used to hate it here but now you make it beautiful for me.

(*Pause. She has lifted her blouse so her breasts show. A rectangle of light is on her torso.*)

It seems I'm always offering these to my lovers. . . . What do you think of my nipples, Nickolas. Too big? Unnatural? They feel unnatural sometimes, but that's why I like them. Andre liked them too. He liked everything about me. My paintings. My body. He liked how I stared at his wife. She has perfect breasts, like mine. Anyway . . . that's why he brought me to Paris. . . . The Louvre bought a painting. Do you think that's good?

(*With a laugh.*)

I got some dough anyway.

(*Pause. She inhales deeply.*)

I'm killing myself with this. It feels so good going down I feel the smoke in my legs. It fills me out. This poison makes me whole. It's like sex that way. Air that turns my insides blue. Breath that pounds my heart. My lips part for that pounding to get between my thighs.

(*She takes another drag,*)

28

I get daydreams about all the lovers I've ever slept with. I keep a hand on my hip, covering the bruises from the needles. A woman pulls it away and rests her lips there. It's always a woman who knows where I need to be kissed.

(*Pause.*)

Want some? No? So professional. Hurry up Nickolas. . . . I'm getting tired. I'm always so tired lately. Will you show everyone these pictures? At least if I'm not remembered for my paintings—someone might remember my breasts.

(*She smiles, takes a deep drag.*)

I love you darling, Nick, almost as much as I love Diego.

HOLY PLACES
Gail Kriegel Mallin

Set in Brooklyn, New York, *Holy Places* explores the prickly relationship between a mother, Helen, and her sensitive but less well-educated daughter, Rona.

Rona, attracted to a handsome, younger man who is boarding with her mother, has asked him if he ever visits his mother's grave. Rona admits she has never been in a cemetery.

RONA: It's discriminating the way they keep all the dead together like that. Locking them away, as if they got nothing more to say.

[**SHANE:** I never thought about it like that.]

RONA: You should be able to bury someone in a place that ain't fenced off, like I seen this man do it once when I was running down the other side of the Loop. He was the biggest, blackest man, I ever seen - in my life - in the whole world! It's real early, ain't even morning yet. No one's around, just me and him. He's way up ahead but I can see he's cradling something in his arm, like maybe a machine gun, I think. And in the other, Jesus, he's carrying a shovel that's big enough to pitch this earth a little closer to the moon. I mean it, it's that big. Well, I figure if I cross over or turn back it might touch him off and maybe he'll mow me right down. So instead, I pretend I don't see him and I keep running, like hell, straight on towards this giant. But when I'm real close you know what I see, Shane? That ain't a machine gun, he's carrying. It's a dog, a little curly black dog. This big man, he's crying. His poor pup is dead, limp, hanging over his arm like a coat. I stopped. It wound up I did the whole thing. So that big man, he dug a grave in the park, put the dog in, shovelled the earth over it. He done it right, you see. Close by, that's where you should bury someone.

HOW SHE PLAYED THE GAME
Cynthia L. Cooper

A series of short, fictional monologues dramatizing the experiences of real sportswomen.

Eleonora Randolph Sears was a very versatile, high-spirited athlete from Boston who lived from the late 1800's to the 1960's. With great humor, she tells how she challenged a women's group who criticized her for wearing trousers.

ELEONORA: I want you to listen to this resolution they passed about me:

"Whereas it has been brought to the attention of the Burlingame Mothers Club . . . "

They're out here in California where the United States Polo Team is practicing. Frankly, I had every intention of becoming the first woman on the team.

" . . . that Miss Eleonora Randolph Sears . . . "

That's me . . . Eleo Sears, great-great-granddaughter of Thomas Jefferson—*the* Thomas Jefferson; the Belle of Boston; and voted the Best Dressed Woman of 1910 . . .

" . . . has been parading through our city in the unconventional trousers and clothes of the masculine sex, having bad effects on the sensibilities of our boys and girls; Now be it resolved that we are strongly opposed to this unsightly mannish garb and request that Miss Sears restrict herself to normal feminine attire.

Signed Mrs. D.S. Harns, the year of 1912."

Naturally, I decided to pay a visit to the Mothers' Club. In trousers!

(*ELEONORA speaks as if addressing the Club.*)

"Dear women. Mothers! Please sit back down. I have no intention of "corrupting" you . . . I haven't that much time. This is my unsightly mannish garb. Take a good look, ladies. Because, *this* is the future staring you straight in the corset!

Your daughters and their daughters won't stand for being laced up, stowed down, braced against a board! And there's more—women are going to leave these silly parlor meetings and play outdoors! Tennis! Biking! Hiking! Polo! In trousers!"

"Ladies, I will make a stand: Women will excel in ways men have not! Not equal. Excel. And to prove it myself, I offer a bet of $200—yes, $200—that I can walk—without stopping—faster and farther than any man has ever done on record. I will walk—from Burlingame to Del Monte, California! One hundred and nine miles! . . . Anyone willing to take my bet?

"Well, then, what a pity. . . . Oh . . . Mrs. D.S. Harns, I believe? You accept my bet? Well, what a bully good opportunity. Then, arrange for your monitors. . . . I will commence at once!"

(ELEONORA *turns as if exiting, begins to strap on her walking shoes, and addresses the audience*.)

One hundred and nine miles is a very long distance. But, I'm no quitter. I'm off.

Five miles. Ten miles. Twenty-five miles. Around about mile 37.1, I'm feeling a little tuckered out. The future of my career as a champion pedestrian doesn't seem too promising.

I promise . . . by George, I promise . . . every time I find out about a woman trying to make a special mark in sports, I will write her a little note. A certain "hey-ho, bully good" congratulations—good luck from me—Eleonora Randolph Sears. I swear to it on this dusty road at mile 37.2 between the cities of Burlingame and Del Monte in the state of California.

(*Conclusion of the opening* ELEONORA *sequence, and the play shifts away from her as the actress transforms into the next character.*)

HOW SHE PLAYED THE GAME
Cynthia L. Cooper

A series of short, fictional monologues dramatizing the experiences of real sportswomen.

Althea Gibson, the first black tennis player to win Wimbledon (male or female), talks about how she got her start in Harlem.

ALTHEA: (*The actress takes on the character of ALTHEA GIBSON. Dresses in tennis whites, hair neatly coifed, she is strong and tough and carries a tennis racquet with a grip that lets everyone know she intends to use it mercilessly. It is July, 1957, and ALTHEA GIBSON is about to become the first black person—male or female—to win the Wimbledon championship. When she speaks, she talks to an off-stage character, Darlene Hard, another tennis player. ALTHEA opens her locker, finds a letter there and reads it.*) "Dear Miss Gibson: Old as I am, I can hardly remember a time when I've been so incensed as I am at the way you've been treated at these so-called tennis tournaments. Well, being the first person—male or female—to break the color barrier is a mighty task. I just want you to know you can count on me rooting my heart out for you whenever you play.

Sincerely: Eleonora Randolph Sears, July, 1957."

That's nice. That's real nice.

(*ALTHEA puts the note down. She looks up as if someone is signalling to her and then calls to Darlene.*)

What?

Hey there! Fifteen minutes to go, Darlene. The ballgirl just came by. You hear me? The match begins in fifteen minutes!

(*ALTHEA picks up the tennis racquet and fiddles with it.*)

It's hot out there, Darlene, honey. Real hot. Nearly a hundred degrees of hot. Folks falling out in the stands. It's so hot they ran out and got blocks of ice to keep the Queen cool. To . . . keep . . . the . . . *Queen* . . . cool. Isn't that something?

So you take care to splash some cold water on your face

before we head out to the court, all right, sugar? I don't want anything happening to you out there today. We got a show to put on for the Queen. Althea Gibson, Darlene Hard . . . two Americans on the grass courts of England.

Me . . . I don't need any cold water. Don't need any ice either. Not today. I'm cool like I've never been. This is the kind of hot we had in Harlem.

Days like today, all of Harlem floats through your memories, pushes out from under your skin like something you can't contain any more. If you listen real close, you can hear the music of Buddy Walker's Harlem Society Orchestra drifting by. And there I am on 143rd Street 'cause in 1939 that's the street the Police Athletic League closed off for us kids to play.

(*She acts out the next scene.*)

"We won! We won! The 143rd Street Club won again!"

"Mr. Walker! Mr. Buddy Walker! Did you see the game? . . . We took the paddle tennis tournament again!

"Phenomenal? You really thought I played phenomenal? Thanks, Buddy. Will you dedicate a song to us tonight? Right on stage?"

"Why do you ask me a question like that? I didn't fight nobody. I didn't have to. I was winning! And the fact is, the story going 'round about me beating up that one boy on the other tennis team isn't true. I only did it because he stole my uncle's five dollars."

"Shoot, Buddy. I don't 'xactly know *how* I learned to play. I just did. They didn't teach us none in school. That's why I had to quit. And my folks don't care none. That's why I had to run away. Now I just play."

"Would I? Yessir, I would love to play at the Harlem River Tennis Courts Club!"

"Yes, sir, I surely do promise."

"Okay, Buddy. I'll say it all the way through. 'If you take me to play at the Harlem River Tennis Courts Club, I . . . promise . . . not to get into any fights.' . . . That aren't absolutely necessary."

I went to the Harlem River Tennis Club, where the fancy Negro society played. It *was* different. Everybody was all dressed up in immaculate white and acted so strange, like it was a church meeting or something. I just walked out on the court and played. Pretty soon all the other players stopped their games and were watching me. I felt grand. I played hard, just like I was on 143rd Street. But, I guess I kind of had a little slipping in my promise to Buddy.

"What do you mean 'out'? That ball was right on the line! Don't tell me that it was out! You tell me to my face that was out!"

(ALTHEA *rushes forward like she's going to fight*.)

Buddy called me over to the sidelines.

"I can't help it, Buddy! The one thing my daddy taught me was how to box. Every time I start losing, I got to fight the other player."

"I understand," he said. "But you don't really know how to fight. Folks have a different way at the Club. Everyone acts polite. They shake hands. And then they go out and play like tigers and beat the liver and lights—out of the ball."

(*Repeating that, gently, as if remembering one of the Ten Commandments*.)

"Shake hands and beat the liver and lights out of the ball."

Not too long after that the two black doctors saw me play. They thought I was the black tennis player who could play in the white tournaments and win. So, they arranged to take me South, where they were from. I went back to high school. Finished, too. At age twenty-one. Went on to college. And all the while I practiced and worked my tennis game like nobody's business.

(*Looks out as if someone's signalling her*.)

What's that? Five more minutes? All right.

Hear that. Darlene? Only five more minutes. Put a washrag to your head. That'll cool you down, doll.

I want to know if you can hear, Darlene? You see, you're white. Harlem's just a name to you. You're still young. About the age I was when I took up tennis. Well, I'm thirty years old, Darlene. That makes me an old lady in tennis.

(*As if playing the game*.)

Last year, the crowd here at Wimbledon booed me, and it threw my game. This year, I'm going to serve hard, let the ball jump off the grass. I'm going to rush the net, cut away the volley. And I won't even notice the heat.

Reason I've been telling you all this, sugar, is, you see, the heat makes me feel right at home. I'm going to win. At last. I've got to, hon. See, I always wanted to be somebody. So what I'm saying, Darlene, is I'm going out there in front of that Queen today, and I'm going to beat the liver and lights out of you. You can understand that, now, can't you, doll?

(Calling.)

Yeah, We're ready.

It'll be over soon, hon. Then we'll go back and win the doubles together—you and me. When we go out there, Darlene, I want you to shake my hand. All right, hon?

(She grabs the note, sticks it in her bag, and turns, with racquet, as if exiting.)

Yeah. We're ready. We're ready.

IN NO MAN'S LAND

Susan Kander

In No Man's Land is set in a ward at the Sunset Ridge Maternity Hospital and Home for Unwed Mothers in Kansas City during the summer of 1919.

Here, Dorothy, a puritanical thirty-nine-year-old legal secretary, describes how she became pregnant.

DOROTHY: . . . It started just after I got the job. My first employer, an eminent attorney in . . . my city died very suddenly and I was let go just as suddenly. I was thirty. Well, who would hire an old maid like me when you can get a pretty young stenographer straight out of school? I was without a job for almost six months! I was so grateful when Mr. G. hired me. I was at my wits end, and the end of my savings. I didn't know what to do—I was so grateful to him. I am an excellent stenographer. Mr. G. is an attorney with the best firm in town . . . He called me in to take a letter one Friday late afternoon shortly after I began working for him, and without ever saying so, it was clear that I was to . . . bend over the desk while he . . . lifted my skirts and he . . . dictated while he. . . . And I . . . I began to cry but I took down . . . every word. My tears blotted my stenobook, I thought he would be angry at me for it, I remember that. It was a letter to a very important client. (*She has another contraction, holds her breath, lets it out.*)

[**ANNABEL:** And that's been going on for nine years?]

DOROTHY: [Every Friday at five fifteen sharp.] He begged my pardon, that first time, for soiling my dress with that revolting stuff. I threw the whole dress away the moment I got home, petticoats and drawers, too! And he told me I had the straightest back he'd ever seen, despite my legs, and that men have "their own peculiar needs—" like that, that's how he described his . . . his bestiality. And I knew, somehow, if I refused, or told anyone—or if I left the job, I would never get a job again.

[**MILLIE:** . . . Didn't you just get used to it, after awhile?]

[**BERNICE:** Millie! Shut up!]

DOROTHY: Never once, in all those years, did he ever look at me! At my face! I wish . . . I wanted . . . If he'd only . . . just one time, at my face. Then I could believe he—actually . . . liked me . . . I'm just his goddamned goat! Oh! Excuse me. I don't normally use curse words. (*She weeps.*)

LADIES
Eve Ensler

Ladies is the poignant story of the difficult lives of various homeless women.

Monetty, a middle-aged   black woman, describes how she met her first husband.

MONETTY: I was born in Ethiopia. I met my husband when I was seven in Newark, New Jersey. My ball went out into the street. He picked up the ball and asked if it was mine. I was very shy. I just nodded. He asked my name and then he asked to be my boyfriend.

Next day we lay down in the grass. I asked him, can you look at the sun without your eyes crying? I kept my eyes wide open, but he couldn't do it. His eyes kept crying out. Juicy tears falling down his mahogany cheeks. He was so tall. So, thin, big, mysterious eyes, kinky hair, smooth skin, sharp Arabian features. Make me explode.

Mr. Mahogany became my husband. We had nine children. FBI said he did a bank robbery. He went to prison for nine years. He was so tall. We used to do it when he was in prison. I waited for him for a long time. He finally came out. He was sleeping next to me one night and he died. I didn't believe it because he was always clowning; playing like he was dead. I started crying and wouldn't stop. I been looking for him since then. Walking the world to find him. He was a monkey man. He used to come home, late at night, after someone had treated him shameful. He'd describe what happened, and then he'd say to me, Gee Monetty, Ain't that a funky way to treat somebody?

LADIES

Eve Ensler

Ladies is the poignant story of the difficult lives of various homeless women.

Nickie, a tough, tattooed woman with a Brooklyn accent and a punk haircut, describes the heavy shopping bag she must carry as representative of all of life's burdens.

NICKIE: You live without walls for too long. It all runs together like raw scrambled eggs. Each part of you bleeds into the other. Your feelings turn into things, shoved into one goddamn, cheap Woolworth bag. You don't even know what's in the bag after a while and you stop caring. All you know is it's heavy and you've got to take it everywhere you go, cos there's no place that wants it. No place that will let you keep it there. And one night you just say fuck it, fuck the bag, and you leave it. And when you go out, you come back after two days and it's gone. You act like you're really pissed off. Who did it, who took my fucking bag. But deep down, you're relieved cos it's gone, and after that, you're gone too in a way, and it feels better. Kind of.

LARDO WEEPING
Terry Galloway

Dinah LaFarge, a short, plump, middle-aged woman, reveals her paranoia and her unique views on employment, society, eating, and the power of the mind in this one-woman show.

Here, Dinah describes an encounter in a trendy restaurant.

DINAH: The last time I ventured out into what you so fancifully call civilized life I went to my favorite bistro. I was sitting at my usual table quietly eating my three entrées when in waltzed the new age Barbie and Ken. They spied me and their eyebrows shot up in horror. "What a disgusting heap of meat," you could hear them thinking, and not just about my entrées. "Such a very conspicuous consumer."

They watched me out of the corners of their eyes as they nibbled on their righteous salads. Then they probably headed home in their gasoline sucking BMW, hopped into a hot tub that uses seven hundred gallons of water a day; hopped out and patted themselves dry with towels that go immediately into the washer/dryer; then he sprays himself down with a huge assortment of aerosols while she touches up her lashes with a wand of mascara that has already been repeatedly poked into some poor rabbit's eye. Then ooh they're feeling sexy. So they give each other a little poke. Seconds later he tosses the condom down the toilet where it heads straight out to sea and promptly strangles some curious dolphin. And they have the nerve to point their fingers at me! I don't even have air conditioning. Is it any wonder I seem like a raving lunatic?

41

LARDO WEEPING

Terry Galloway

Dinah LaFarge, a short, plump, middle-aged woman, reveals her paranoia and her unique views on employment, society, eating, and the power of the mind in this one-woman show.

Here, Dinah expresses her dislike for power.

DINAH: There was only one time in my life that I was truly without question one of the majority. I was nine, I was a member of a gang—a gang of marauding boys as it were. That was probably because when I was nine I was a bit like Little Lotta. Unbelievably strong. And since I could beat the shit out of the boys and I had the requisite foul mouth they quickly embraced me as one of them. Well one day we boys set out to capture a girl. So we captured a weak one. And we all took turns sitting on top of her. The idea was to get on top of her, hold her down, kiss her hard enough to get her mouth open and then let go with a huge gob of spit. That was all. So we were all taking turns sitting on top of her and her mouth was full of spit and she was terrified, crying for her mother . . . but who was listening. And then it was my turn. I had enjoyed the comraderie up until then . . . I'd been sucking on my cheeks trying to get the longest, drooling piece of spit ready—it was a contest by then. But when I sat down on top of her I realized that I knew her. Oh, I didn't really know her. But I knew the look in her eyes . . . I knew the look in her eyes.

Power makes me uneasy I suppose. Just not quite ruthless enough.

LATE BUS TO MECCA
Pearl Cleage

This play is set in a Greyhound Bus Terminal in Detroit, Michigan in 1970. Ava Johnson is a twentyish black woman who is headed to Atlanta to see the triumphant return to the ring of Muhammed Ali after three years of exile as a conscientious objector to the Vietnam War. Although a prostitute, Ava represents all black women and their "potential for . . . salvation".

While waiting for a friend who is supposed to go to Atlanta with her, Ava paints her toenails and chatters to another black woman who looks abused but never speaks.

AVA: (*AVA is painting her toenails carefully. She has cotton balls in between her toes. She is quiet, concentrating on her work. ABW's eyes are closed. AVA finishes and screws the top back on the bottle, looking at her toes with satisfaction.*) They talking about snow up here next week and it's still Indian summer down South. Sandal weather! (*She blows on her toes.*) You going to Atlanta, too?

(*ABW looks at AVA. Panic.*)

Relax, honey. I don't care where you're going, okay? You don't have to get paranoid. Is somebody after you? (*ABW doesn't respond, but does look at AVA.*)

Well, more power to you, honey. It's every woman for herself, I say. When it's time to make a move, make a move. (*AVA fans her nails with her hands and blows on them.*) I've never been any further south than D.C. Sherri hasn't either. She grew up in D.C., but she said as soon as she could, she went north. I hope it's not too country down there. I hate country. Tony had a friend who lived way out. I thought the nigga was hiding from somebody, but Tony said he just couldn't stand no whole bunch of noise since he got back from Vietnam.

He had these big old bug eyes, too. Always trying to talk up on something and his damn eyes getting bigger and bigger. . . .

But Atlanta's spose to be a big city, so we'll see.

(*AVA looks around again for SHERRI.*)

She is really getting on my nerves with this shit. Sometimes I start thinking about all the stuff I don't like about my girl and I say, so what do you like about her? And it's there, but it's so much harder to put into words, you know?

Don't get me started thinking about that shit! We got 22 hours between here and Atlanta I do not want to ride that far being evil.

I hate riding the bus by myself. It's okay when you got somebody with you, but when you're by yourself, there's always a nigga with a hard on grinning up in your face, 'scuse my French.

(*ABW closes her eyes again and leans back weakly.*)

(*Gently.*) You really look bad, honey. Are you on something?

LETTERS HOME
Rose Leiman Goldemberg

As seen through the eyes of Aurelia Plath, *Letters Home* reveals much about the life of her daughter, Sylvia Plath, the brilliant and often controversial poet. The play is structured as both a dialogue between mother and daughter, which takes place in Aurelia's mind, and letters that Sylvia wrote to her mother.

Aurelia, speaking as the seventeen-year-old Sylvia, reveals her girlish dreams and trepidations for the future.

AURELIA SPEAKING AS SYLVIA: (*A decision. To herself, to* SYLVIA, *to the audience; gathering resolution, strength.*) November 13, 1949. As of today I have decided to keep a diary again—just a place to write my thoughts and opinions when I have a moment. Somehow I have to keep and hold the rapture of being *seventeen*. Every day is so precious. I feel infinitely sad at the thought of all this time melting farther and farther away from me as I grow older. *Now, now* is the perfect time of my life.

I still do not know myself. Perhaps I never will. But I feel free—unbound by responsibility, I still can come up to my own private room, with my drawings hanging on the walls, and pictures pinned up over the bureau—a room suited to me, uncluttered and peaceful. I love the quiet lines of the furniture, the two bookcases filled with poetry books and fairy tales saved from childhood.

Always I want to be an observer. I want to be affected by life deeply, but never so blinded that I cannot see my share of existence in a wry, humorous light.

I am afraid of getting older. I am afraid of getting married. Spare me from cooking three meals a day—spare me from the relentless cage of routine and rote. I want to be *free*—free to know people and their backgrounds—free to move to different parts of the world. I want, I think, to be omniscient. I think I would like to call myself "the girl who wanted to be God" . . .

perhaps I am *destined* to be classified and qualified. But, oh, I cry out against it. I am I.

I love my flesh, my face, my limbs. I have erected in my mind an image of myself, idealistic and beautiful. Is not that image, free from blemish, the true self—the true perfection? (Oh, even now I glance back on what I have just written—how foolish it sounds, how overdramatic!)

Never, never, never will I reach the perfection
I long for with all my soul.

There will come a time when I must face myself at last. Even now I dread the big choices
which loom up in my life. I am afraid. I feel uncertain. I am not as wise as I have thought.

I can now see, as from a valley, the roads lying open for me
but I cannot see the end—the consequences.

Oh, I love *now*, with all my fears and forebodings,
for now I still am not completely molded. *I am strong.*

My life is just beginning!

MAGGIE AND MISHA
Gail Sheehy

Margaret Thatcher, ex-Prime Minister of Great Britain, has a momentous meeting with then-Soviet Premier Gorbachev. Gradually, as they cut through politics and policy, they connect on a human level.

Here, Maggie relates a humiliating experience that formed her determination to succeed.

THATCHER: I was once invited for a weekend party by the son of an earl. (*She stands and acts out this reverie with dramatic gestures.*) My mother sewed me a dress. Neat but dull. He did come to collect me in a Rolls, and you can imagine, the son of a lord, it was like stepping into another world—where people never have to introduce themselves, or finish their sentences. Oh, and he gave me the most exquisite bouquet of roses. Made quite a fuss over me. But when it came to drive me home, he sailed right past me—with another girl in the Rolls!

[**GORBACHEV:** No, the rogue!]

THATCHER: (*Whispery, pained.*) Turns out, he had mistaken her for me. He didn't even know the *difference* between me and some other girl. Very hurtful. I went home on the train, alone, those beautiful roses without a drop of water, just withering to death in my lap. "Well, Margaret Hilda," I told myself, "you don't want to be like *any* of them—the girls or the boys. No matter what, you are going to be *memorable.*"

MILK OF PARADISE
Sallie Bingham

Set in 1951, *Milk of Paradise* is a coming-of-age story of an aristocratic, Southern family. Missy, a restless, dreamy fourteen year old, longs to escape from her stifling, provincial environment.

While undressing a doll, Missy describes what it is like to be "felt up."

Missy: (*Beginning to undress doll.*) They go for the button first, at the top, under the collar. Then they go down to the second button and the third and all the time, you're telling them, No! You can feel their fingers through the material, you can feel their nails slide on the little pearl buttons. They're not quick about it. Then you start to say, No, again, real loud—and argue. Sometimes they answer you back and then you can get them off the track with an argument about the way people ought to behave, about RESPECT. Other times they don't even bother to answer you, they just go right on. You can't argue by yourself, that's no distraction. (*She unbuttons the doll's skirt.*) Then they get down to the waist and they start to undo your skirt. If you've got on your school uniform, they have to hitch their fingers inside the waistband to get a purchase on that big button. Of course if it's hot weather, after school time, and you've got your shorts on, that makes it easier. Soon as they get that button undone, they put their fingers in and feel your skin. They say, Ooh—you hear them draw their breath. They're feeling your skin—it's cool, it's smooth, they say it feels like silk. You don't need to go on arguing, then, you just need to lie still and listen to them saying, Ooh, Ooh. . . . (*She speaks in a sharply practical voice as she takes off the doll's skirt.*) You don't have any underwear on, Darling! How can you go out in public with nothing over your weewee? (*She turns the doll over and spanks it.*) Spank you, Darling, for your own good. It hurts me more than it hurts you.

MILLIE
Susan J. Kander

Millie tells the story of a funny, courageous, black woman who, for eleven years, has taken care of her severely brain-damaged husband.

Millie, a grandmother who adores the singer, Teddy Pendergrass, describes how she rearranges her life to go to one of his concerts with her old friend, Sam.

MILLIE: I should have known Sam was low class right from the beginning when he offered me my choice between last row at Teddy Pendergrass and ring-side seats at All-star Wrestling. I knew he wanted me to choose wrestling, too! Almost did, too, just to make him like me. But I got hold of myself. I said, "Mildred, what are you doing? He's giving you a choice: choose right." You would never of pulled that kind of stunt, I know that. You would of said "Kick off your house shoes, Sugar; we are stepping out." Like you did remember when you took me to the Mark IV and we dined and we danced all night long— . . . Listen to yourself, Mildred. Eleven years and listen to you. Dear God. Well, nothing stops the sand, Baby. Someday, somehow, it'll be better, ain't that right? . . . That was the first time I ever slipped out on you, long after the first surgery. I don't think it troubled Sam none, in fact I know it didn't. But it troubled me plenty and I wasn't going to do it for no All-star Wrestling! Not even Gorgeous George versus The Stomper! Yes, I said The Stomper, Honey, he's our man, yes I know; Millie know. No, it ain't on now; You already watched it today, come on at noon, remember? You watched it with Charles, when he come by to give you your lunch. It ain't on again 'til Monday.

(She has returned to vanity, and resumes with make-up and jewelry.)

Perry'll be by later on after I go. He'll sit with you watch the ball game, okay? Give you your dinner. He called me yesterday, asked could he come by and see his daddy, since he didn't feel like going out on no hot dates. (*Laughs.*) That old Perry. My baby some smart kid, ain't he? Smart? He's downright crafty. Twenty-three years old, junior college graduate, and ain't got no babies! Ain't even shacking with no one; and furthermore, ain't even looking for it. Now that's a crafty kid. Must of took a good lesson from Charles and Tony and all they babies. But imagine that, Honey: of all my boys, my baby a college graduate, working two jobs, money in his pants and ain't got no one to spend it on but his own self. And his old Mama, of course. He gave me these earrings, remember? And for no good reason, neither. Didn't even want me to feed him dinner or nothing.

(*Fetching shoes out of a closet.*)

I can't believe it. I told them all three a million times, and you heard me say it: "You make babies, you keep them at your house. I'll visit, on Sundays, after church. Put your lady on the pill; wear a raincoat; do whatever you got to do 'cause I ain't bringing up your children. I'm tired." Now what do I get every morning but BANG goes the screen door and "Hey Grammaw, got any chocolate cake today?" (*Laughs.*) That baby Tony is so fat already, he's just a little butterball. . . . I'll never know what went right with Perry, but he's as free as an eagle that boy. I ain't been that free since I was dragging the chair up to the cupboard and reaching my dirty little hand into Mama's sugarbowl. And even that wasn't free, 'cause she sent me out to pick my own switch for the whipping every time! (*Laughs.*) ...Your mama ain't sent so much as a pair of pajamas in eleven years. She don't care if I was to put you away in a nursing home. And she sure as hell ain't about to help pay for it.

(*Sitting beside bed, putting on shoes.*)

Dr. Brackett started in about a home before you was even out of the hospital the first time, all 67 pounds of you. But he dried up about it when you started gaining weight for me. Then, after the second surgery, and the strokes, couldn't nobody understand you but me, and I said to him "How's anybody going to understand him when he's asking for his orange pop, or for the channel to be switched, or trying to tell somebody he done stooled in his bed again? No thank you, he stays home with me. I got my boys to help me out. They call him Daddy, you know, ever since we got married, me and Honey. So he stays home. . . . Two major surgeries, more strokes than I got fingers, and now all these seizures: Lord, Honey, how much can a person put up with huh? Ain't you tired yet? You got nothing left hardly but a mouth, and not even one good eye. Ain't you plain tired? How many more nights like last night, Honey, huh? I can't afford enough sets of sheets for you, and I get so tired of doing laundry in the middle of the night. Dear God, when are you going to get tired? Just plain wore out? . . . No, why would you? All you do is sit up in that bed all day, watch TV and eat up my kitchen. You're happy. . . . You know, you don't even look like the Honey I married . . .

(*Rising, going back to vanity.*)

I guess I don't look too much like the Sugar you married any more, now, do I? These black bags under my eyes. Hair needs touching up. I don't like my roots showing like that. Honey? What do you really think about this dress? Kind of makes me look like a . . . billboard, don't it? (*Laughs.*) I want Teddy to think I'm sexy.

(*She puts on a belt that transforms the dress from sack to dynamite.*)

And old Sam can just run it out his ass if he say one damn word that ain't a compliment about this dress. I know I said sweet words, but that's okay, it ain't Sunday yet. No sir, it ain't Sunday yet. I got all of Saturday night just waiting for me and Teddy. And then I'll think about Sam, old two-timing lizard. He just got to stay cool and wait for me, 'cause I promised myself I'm going to take myself backstage afterward and personally wish Mr. Teddy Pendergrass the best of luck and God bless him for the rest of his life. They better let me in back there, too: anybody get in my way I'll just sit on them—Boom!

(*Lights changing, she is leaving the bedroom and going backstage at the theater.*)

'Cause I'm going to see my Teddy, tell him "I'll drive your wheelchair any time you in town. You just keep singing, Mister; you keep on living, 'cause you can't afford to stop turn around look behind you, see how nice things used to be. You just keep your eyes going forward; look on ahead now. You keep singing your songs 'cause I want to hear them. I always want to keep hearing them, Teddy, you understand me? Always and always . . . "

(*Lights return to normal, she is back home.*)

Never look behind you. Never ever. That's what I'm going to tell Mr. Teddy Pendergrass when I see him tonight backstage at the Uptown Theater—

PARALLAX
(IN HONOR OF DAISY BATES)
Denise Hamilton

Parallax illuminates key moments in the life of Daisy Bates, the heroic teacher who fought for integration in Little Rock, Arkansas in the 1950's.

Here, Daisy, addressing a large group of people, reveals why she feels no bitterness over the consequences of standing up for what she believes in.

DAISY: (*At a podium.*) During my speaking engagements these past few years, I am often asked how I felt that day in 1957 the paratroopers arrived. President Eisenhower had responded to our telegram earlier so I knew what to expect. The kids were all gathered at my house—we had decided they should leave from there. When Minnijean looked out of the window and saw the soldiers coming she said "For the first time I feel like an American. Somebody cares about me." There were 22 soldiers immediately surrounding the kids; 2,300 more with gas masks and bayonets lining the street up to the school. I was excited the troops were sent, but not happy. Any time it takes 11,000 soldiers to assure nine Negro children their constitutional rights in a democratic society, I can't be happy.

People also expect me to be bitter about . . . my personal life. You see my husband L.C. and I lost our newspaper. The paper's advertisers cancelled their contracts, for no mysterious reason, and with them went sixteen years of our lives. I truly understand the power of advertisers and the control media has in choosing what's presented. Which is why the success of the State Press as an activist paper meant so much to us. We've had all the bad experiences of civil rights workers: being arrested, being threatened, and so forth. However, at some point you pass over the crisis. I don't know why you do. But when you've passed it a lot of things are lost in your new perspective. They're not important anymore. What is important is that through that outrage at Little Rock the world was made to realize the shameful discrimination that has been practiced in this country, even against young children. If they could, most people would just sit back, or be fence sitters. But each and every man and woman can make a difference if he or she believes they can; if they've had someone to help them; one person to tell them they can. We've all got our own resources we can use, to build on, and it doesn't always take money or contacts, but just plain energy that's focused.

Events in history occur when the time has ripened for them—but they need a spark.

PERSONALITY
Gina Wendkos and Ellen Ratner

Personality is a one-woman play with many characters, primarily Ellen, a young, single woman in New York who is trying to find herself, and Lorette, Ellen's overbearing, Jewish mother who wants Ellen to have a good personality so she can get a man.

Here, Ellen wistfully describes one type of woman she would like to be.

ELLEN: The thing I always wanted to be called was a HOT BITCH. There was something very sexy, very dirty, very Italian about that. I wanted it. I wanted to wake up one morning with some guy and hear him on the phone. Some guy named Jake or Rick. I wanted to lie in bed, leave the sheets draped so that only my thighs were covered. I'd lie there pretending to be asleep, but really I've got it arranged so I look takeable. Very takeable. I'll move my hair so that it covers the pillow but still shows my face and I'd lift up my hips so my waist looks smaller just like in the photos and I'll listen to this Jake or Rick or Tony guy on the phone, talking to one of his friends. "Hey, buddy, how ya doin'? Listen I've got this really hot bitch here. Yeah, she steams. Huh? Her name is Ellen, and she looks like a Sophia Loren type. One of those round hot Italians. Nah, met her on the street and I just wanted her. I couldn't stay away. So I went up to her and said I've never seen anyone like you, I've never smelled anyone like you, I've never wanted anyone like you, and she just looked at me and smiled. I knew I could touch her and I knew once I touched her I'd never leave. Yeah, she's really something else. I could get lost in her hair alone, it's so long and gets everywhere but I want my mouth on it." That's the kind of conversation I imagine. Then this Jake or Rick or Tony guy would come in and see me posed like that. Even if he knows it's arranged he'll like it. He'll come in and pull the sheet back and I'll stay still and he'll just look at me and I can feel his eyes, his wanting me, so I'll let out a little moan so he'll know I'm awake. (*Phone ring.*) Fuck the personality for a minute. Sometimes I want to be wanted for just the way I walk.

55

PERSONALITY
Gina Wendkos and Ellen Ratner

Personality is a one-woman play with many characters, primarily Ellen, a young, single woman in New York who is trying to find herself; and Lorette, Ellen's overbearing, Jewish mother who wants Ellen to have a good personality so she can get a man.

Ellen reveals her frustration over both her lack of money and The City's emphasis on the importance of having money.

ELLEN: Money. Sure, got lots of it. Can't you tell? Don't I have that certain swagger that a New York woman has? It's a casual stride. It's a slow walk, but one that gets where it has to be. Slow yet quick. Y'know what I mean? I never understood how to have money . . . the idea of becoming a career girl always seemed so stupid to me . . . of all the stupid advances of women, that has got to be the worst. Sure Lois Lane, she's got a byline in the Metro paper, she cooks quick dinners and still has time to fly all night with her boyfriend. What the hell is so liberating about leaving the home and kids for some stupid desk job . . . some idiot paper work job that men used to do? But now women get to because we're oh, so advanced. That's bullshit. So that's why I never figured out how to have money, and in this city that's ridiculous, because that's exactly how people judge you here. By your apartment, by your clothes, by your shoes. Shoes are very important because they're so expensive, the good ones, and the bad ones are a dead giveaway that you're piss poor. So I do what any noncareer, nonmarried girl would do, spend forty bucks for expensive sneakers and then everyone will think that you can afford expensive shoes . . . but choose not to. Money. Growing up it wasn't hip to want it. Who knew that would only be a 10-minute trend. Now every street bum, every street scum, every low life standing on the corner has more cash than I have. And I haven't got the first clue.

PERSONALITY
Gina Wendkos and Ellen Ratner

Personality is a one-woman play with many characters, primarily Ellen, a young, single woman in New York who is trying to find herself; and Lorette, Ellen's overbearing, Jewish mother who wants Ellen to have a good personality so she can get a man.

Ellen points out some of the contradictions that society has placed on females.

ELLEN: Oh yeah, a woman . . . do you get it? You know, that other group that's not a man but also not a teenager. No giggling allowed. Pretty strict rules in this woman biz. As a kid it never mattered, you could climb trees and giggle. But now only one of those attitudes is allowed or you don't get over. It's OK. If you want to act tough. . . . "HEY, WHAT THE FUCK YOU MEAN" . . . then people know who you are . . . oh, she's a tough broad, watch out. And it's cool if you have pert breasts and giggle, then people know the score. But try having pert breasts, saying "FUCK OFF" and giggling. People look at you like, "Huh, aren't you breaking a few rules?" If you're the tough type you're supposed to have saggy tits used mainly for childbearing . . . and if you're the giggling type your breasts are meant for handling, open invitation . . . but try having saggy tits and giggling . . . the game's up. I mean, these are invisible rules. But watch. Look out, and see if I'm right, giggling is forgiven if the girl is hot, and tough is forgiven if she isn't. But make a sexy girl tough and no one knows the right response. Then all of a sudden men start stuttering and tripping and losing their grip. All of a sudden you're a prickteaser 'cause their dicks are getting hard, and they say, "WHY THE SHIT DOES SHE HAVE TO WEAR THOSE HEELS?" you hear them say. But the giggly types can with no problem. So you see, some days I'm a giggly type. I laugh at everything. I'm coy. I'm sweet. I'm available. And other days I'm a tough broad. Take no shit.

Gotta get the job done, gotta get it going. But my tits stay the same. That's where things get pretty confusing for the world at large.

PERSONALITY
Gina Wendkos and Ellen Ratner

Personality is a one-woman play with many characters, primarily Ellen, a young, single woman in New York who is trying to find herself; and Lorette, Ellen's overbearing, Jewish mother who wants Ellen to have a good personality so she can get a man.

This is a "tour de force" monologue with Ellen "becoming" each of many distinctive personalities, trying them on for size to see if any of them fits. All she really wants is to be accepted for herself.

ELLEN: (*On phone.*) Hello. No, Mama, he didn't call . . . how the fuck do I know? Huh, are you satisfied . . . you said he wouldn't and he didn't. So do you have the balloons out?? Are you throwing a party? Huh? Did you make a fuckin' cake while you're at it? No, no! I'll say whatever I want at this fucking point. I am sick and tired of hearing how I should do it, how I should say it, how I should act it . . . are you gonna show me how to fuck, too? Who are they, who are them? Bullshit! My personality, Ma. WHAT IS WRONG WITH MY PERSONALITY? WHO DO YOU WANT ME TO BE? HUH? WHO?

GAME SHOW LADY: (*Midwest accent.*) I'm going to be on the 10,000 Dollar Pyramid. I'm so excited. You see I read everything. Books, magazines, backs of cereal boxes. Just ask me anything. (*Announcer's voice.*) "What is the capital of Burma?" (*Buzz.*) "Rangoon." "How does the whojoo bird protect itself?" "Its fur inflates into a protective covering." I know it all. Animal, vegetable, and mineral. They also like me on TV because I have a bubbly personality. So when they say, "You have won a trip to Puerta Viarta! (*ELLEN jumps up from sitting—stage flooded in wash.*) Does that come with the Samsonite? Oh my God! I know just what I'm going to wear . . . my red dress. You can't wear strips and plaids because they bleed, that's TV talk. I love TV talk. And I'm going to get my hair done and buy new shoes, then watch out America. I'm gonna take you for every red cent you have.

Spanish Cha-Cha Girl: (*Low-class Spanish accent.*) Maria, conyo, Julio, si. I love this place. Mongo Santa Maria (*Dances and sings.*) Julio get me a gin and tonic. Julio, he's my boyfriend. He's got the best ass in the place. He wears his pants real tight, too. He likes it when I wear this red band-aid top. But when you're dancing it keeps falling down so you have to keep a whooping and a whooping. Julio and I are going to be in a contest and we're going to win. Julio thinks the prize is fifty dollars but I'm going to surprise him. The prize is going to be me. And I'm not going to use birth control. So that way I get the ring, the car, and Julio.

Video Girl: (*Brooklynese accent.*) Hey, hi guys, hi Rusty. How ya doin'? Slap me five. Sally, Sally you look gorgeous. Let me see this dress. Hey, who's the squirt at my machine? Looks right for you Sal, about nine or ten years old. Hi Pee Wee. How ya doin'? Oh boy, 500 points, I don't believe it. Better watch out, you're gonna be eaten. Better watch out. Told you. You're history. OK, the champ is here. (*Makes the sound of Pac Man.*) See I do this game better than I know anything else. See. All these people are gonna gather 'round me now. Watch. Here comes that Reggie guy. He's cute, but obnoxious. Hi Reggie. I cut last period. School is boring. Yeah, I got 50,000 points and I've only been here 30 seconds. OK. I'll see you around. Creep. People say I could go pro at this game. Then I could quit school. What do I have to know about the Boston Tea Party? I don't even drink tea.

Miss America: (*Dumb southern drawl. Sings "Here she comes, Miss America."*) Thank you all, thank you so much. It's been a wonderful year being Miss America. And now I am giving my crown to the new Miss America. Whoever she is I'm sure she won't have a year like I've had. I won a college scholarship. . . . What? . . . and a movie contract. . . . What? . . . and a trip around the world . . . the crown, I know. I traveled around the world and saw so many underprivileged people. You should see how these poor darlin's live. They have animals right in the house, this yak came right up to the table and ate off it. It was disgusting. And the men have the longest (*Said in silence.*) you ever saw. I remember we were in some remote part of Africa and there was this little boy and he didn't have any shoes. Well my heart was just pained, so, I turned to my manager and said "What can we do?" Well, he turned to me and said "Karen Ann Sue, I ain't doing shit." So I turned to that little native and said (*Sings.*) "We are the world, we are the children." That's just one of the many things I've done as Miss America. Let's hope the new Miss A. will be generous and kind. Thank you.

HOUSEWIFE: (*Nancy Reagan accent*) I take pride in the things I do. Every single one of them. Some women keep their homes in horrible condition. They leave the butter out and it sours. They serve jelly from the jar and it develops an unsightly crust around the rim. Oh yes, and they use paper napkins. REALLY! Paper napkins. (*Screams at kids.*) TOMMY, JIMMY, GET AWAY FROM THAT REFRIGERATOR BEFORE I CUT YOUR HANDS OFF. I use cloth napkins only. I have several patterns. Checkers, strips, floral prints, even polka dots. But of course polka dots I only use in summer. Really, polka dots in winter. (*Screams at kids.*) DID YOU HEAR WHAT I SAID? DID YOU HEAR WHAT I SAID? GET UPSTAIRS WITH YOUR BROTHER. Ah, summertime, such a peaceful season. The little misters are in camp. The birds are in the yard. Robert's buzzing like a bee. The polka dots are in bloom again. What a pretty pattern.

WAITRESS: (*White-trash urban accent.*) We got a burger travelin' and a Mr. Potato on a sidecar. Hi, hon, coffee? How you doin' today? What's it gonna be? Whole wheat, white or rye? Cole slaw or french fries? Anything to drink? Coke. Here you go, Chan, couple of orders at a time. I run this counter like clockwork. By the time they have their cigarettes out of their pocket I get a cup of java in front of their face. (*Ding.*) When I hear that bell I run. I don't care what anyone says anything made with cheese gets soggy under these lights. OK we got a tuna melt, cheeseburger, tuna on rye, cheeseburger. And to drink? Coffee, coffee, sanka. I have a lot of miles on these feet. I got everything. Corns, callouses, bunions. Real pretty let me tell you. But when my customers come in they know they're gonna get quick courteous service. Not many people give you that at all.

OPERA LADY: (*Pretentious actress accent.*) Excuse me, miss. Miss. Miss, may I please have a toasted bagel, a fruit cup, and a tea with lemon. No butter on the bagel, please. You see, I'm an opera singer and it creates too much mucous. You see, I'm with the 78th Street Upper West Side Opera Folly. It's a very reputable Opera Folly and I'm a founding member. I'm their only female tenor. We're in rehearsal right now for "Carmen" and guess who I'm going to be. Guess. Guess. Guess. Guess. Guess. Carmen! It has my favorite aria! (*Sings.*) But I also like pop songs. (*Sings.*) My love's in jeopardy, baby, ooh, ooh, tom tom toma tom tom tom. Excuse me miss, but could you turn down the air conditioning, I think it's blowing on the back of my neck. Miss, I told you no butter on the bagel. (*Starting to get mad.*) You don't have any fruit cup. Why didn't you tell me sooner? You've just wasted my time. I'm busy in rehearsal.

(*Medley and frenzy of characters—this blends into a cacophony of all characters until final frenzy—woman switches accents and characters.*)

GAME SHOW LADY: Uh, uh. (*Buzz.*) Kentucky. Tennessee? I always get that one right.

SPANISH CHA-CHA GIRL: What do you mean you're dancing with someone else Julio? You motherfucker I'm gonna kill you.

VIDEO GIRL: Hey, what's the matter with this machine? I never lose my quarter. Where's the guy?

MISS AMERICA: Let me keep the crown just one more year. I promise I'll give it back. Just one more year.

HOUSEWIFE: I only have paper napkins. I only have paper napkins.

WAITRESS: What do you mean my coffee is bitter? This is a fresh pot. Why don't you go somewhere else buddy?

OPERA LADY: I told you no butter on my bagel. The mucous is already forming. Just get me the check. (*Cough, choke.*)

(*Fade lights—frenzy.*)

GAME SHOW LADY: (*Buzz.*) Don't I get the . . .

SPANISH CHA-CHA GIRL: (*Buzz.*) Julio you son of a bit . . .

VIDEO GIRL: (*Buzz.*) Hey Rusty, hey watch me now . . .

MISS AMERICA: (*Buzz.*) Don't take my crown, don't take my . . .

HOUSEWIFE: (*Buzz.*) Napkins, napkins . . . I uh . . .

WAITRESS: (*Buzz.*) Coffee bitter, my coffee . . . why I'll . . .

OPERA LADY: (*Sing, sing.*) SING.

(*Frenzy flip-out–shaking–etc. Pause, breathe. After flip-out, woman sits serenely in chair, wash out. Lights up where ELLEN sits.*)

(Switch to ELLEN.)

ELLEN: In America, you look around and you see all these images of people who you should be. People with long hair down to their waist, people with eyes that sparkle, people with clever accents, people who tell witty stories, people that have courage, people that make shyness an art form. There are so many images of people to choose from. Sure, I always wanted to be famous. Who doesn't? It's not just from you Ma. It's from the children on their swings, from the old people shrinking in Miami Beach, it's from the magazines, from the posters, from the airwaves. It's everywhere . . . everywhere, telling me to have friends I haven't deserved, find lovers to be slaves, keep my phones ringing forever. Isn't that right? Huh, Ma? Don't we all? FAME AND HEAT AT THE TOP. Just like you said. They'll watch you, they'll imitate you, they'll like you, for your hair, for your smile, for your figure. I don't want to be a spider anymore, some slimy thing crawling around people's teeth. I don't want to become saliva that gets spit out. Saliva that lands in the gutter under the feet of witty people. I want to take the magazine images out of my head the` way some people take out the garbage. Don't you see Ma? I want the little things, things I can understand. I don't know what to do with the big things anymore, the things I keep tripping over, the couches, the big couches sitting in the middle of my living room that I can't move, that I can't budge until I start crying and screaming for the little things. A piece of corn I can understand, but what is personality? Huh Ma? What is a personality? So, I said to the Frenchmen in the cafes, the Italians in the gondolas, to the Indians on the reservations, so I said to her, I'm lazy, I'm sloppy, and I have flat feet. Take me or leave me. Hopefully she'll take me.

RELATIVITY

Marlane G. Meyer

Relativity describes the strange relationship which exists among three people, Carl, a scientist of some kind, Carmen, his wife, and Carmen's friend, Lucy. Carl lives in a scientific fantasy world, listening to tapes of himself speaking on relativity, and watching the Playboy channel. His wife dominates him in a peculiar, passive-aggressive alliance.

Here, at the end of the play, Carmen, (40s), has completely dominated her husband and is enjoying humiliating him.

CARMEN: (*CARL is sitting in front of the television watching the Playboy channel. He wears a robe. He is impassive. His face is a void. Carmen enters with a bucket of water, soap, and a wash rag. She turns off the television. She pulls the robe off his shoulders. She begins to wash his face. First with soap, then rinsing, one small area at a time, working her way down his neck to his chest.*) Is that too hot? No? Perfect . . . okay. (*Beat.*) So . . . I was sitting there . . . and I was listening, which is all I do when I eat lunch with her, she talks and I listen. And I was staring out the window . . . watching . . . because there is the airport . . . and you can watch the planes fly, little planes. You can see them take off and land. Well, I was watching one little plane coming in . . . when I saw another little plane cross in front of it. I barely had time to say . . . oh no . . . but that the planes had crashed and made the most beautiful ball of flame. Fire looking, orange, red and bright white yellow. They came down in the street in front of the restaurant. I didn't know what to do, I decided to finish my meal. They'd made my hamburger too rare, it was a particular shade of pink I don't find appetizing, but I ate it anyway. After lunch, I decided to stay. I'd never seen a crash. I walked to a building with windows that looked down on the crash sight, I climbed the stairs and watched while they pulled the planes apart. I guess they were looking for survivors. I wasn't sure. A man came up behind me and said two of the people had been found on the roof of an office building . . . burned beyond recognition. As he was talking I saw them pull something large and pink out of the wreckage. No arms or legs . . . no head? No way to distinguish front from back? His clothes had apparently been burned off. He lay in the street the same particular shade of pink as my undercooked hamburger patty. I thought to myself, what a coincidence. Pretty soon a large trailer came to pick up the plane, then the coroner's van arrived to get the body. And guess what? The coroner's van . . . was the same, very same particular shade of pink as my hamburger and the headless torso of the pilot. I don't know that I have ever felt more fully alive, more fully in touch with the law of synchronicity . . .

(*She stops, she smiles, pats him, she takes a towel and dries his head off very hard, she rubs his skin till he's pink. He doesn't react. She finishes, she pulls his robe up, ties it.*)

You're so lucky you never learned to fly. You're an earth sign, you wouldn't be safe in a plane. You'd probably end up a headless pink torso on black asphalt. Earth people should travel by train. Safer. You know? Clackety, clackety, clackety, clackety, clackety, clackety, clackety, clackety, clackety, clackety, clackety, clackety, clackety, clackety . . . how soothing. Sitting in the railway carriage, watching the embankment go by.

It's difficult to know whether you're moving at all. Maybe it's really the embankment that's moving? Hmmm? Huh? Huh?

SCENE OF SHIPWRECK
Pamela Mills

Daphne, thirties, and Ruth, late twenties, live with their parents, who exercise strict control over their daughters, in rural South Africa.

Here, Daphne describes an argument with her abusive ex-husband to her sister.

DAPHNE: When we first met, Robert was so sweet. He used to bring me flowers every time. He was always so considerate. Once I was wearing a dress and he said, "I don't think you should be wearing that." I said, "But it's the fashion—everyone's wearing this kind of thing this summer." And he put his arms around me, and kissed my neck and said, "You're not everyone. You're my special girl. Do it just for me." And he was so sweet and gentle, I did it. Just to please him. (*Pause.*)
One time we were going somewhere. And just as we were leaving, I remembered I had to phone a friend—Irene—to make an arrangement with her. She wasn't at home. She was at her boyfriend Jonathan's, so I called her there, and he answered the phone. We spoke a little while, then Irene came to the phone. I'd been out with Jonathan a few times and Robert hated him and that whole crowd. "Full of nonsense," he said, "They think they're a cut above the rest of us." When I got off the phone he was in such a temper. "Just get in the car," he yelled and slammed the door. As he drove, he got more and more worked up. "All I hear these days is Jonathan Jonathan Jonathan," he screamed. I just sat there. I didn't know what to do, what to say. He was being so unreasonable. Then he hit me. With the back of his hand, across the face. While he was driving. I was so . . . I'd never seen him like that before. I mean he'd been jealous, but never like that. So I just sat there. I didn't say a word, I was so shocked, and the tears began to roll down my face, and I couldn't stop them, and the more I couldn't make them stop, the angrier I got. I was sobbing and sobbing and I

couldn't look at him. . . . I felt so . . . humiliated. And then he pulled the car over and stopped. I turned to look at him—I wasn't sure what he was going to do. He had tears in his eyes, he was crying himself. He said he was sorry, would I forgive him, he'd never do it again. He looked so pathetic. I believed him.

STILL LIFE
Emily Mann

Set in 1978 and based upon actual interviews, *Still Life* examines three people who have, in one way or another, been deeply affected by the Vietnam War.

Cheryl, (30s), an abused wife and a "survivor," describes why she stays with Mark, her abusive husband.

CHERYL: I'm scared knowing that I have to keep my mouth shut.
I don't know this for a fact, but I mean
I fantasize a lot.
I have to.
I've got nothing else to do.
See, I've got no real line of communication at all, on this issue.
If I ever told him I was scared for my life, he'd freak out.
If I ever said anything like that how would he react?
Would he get angry?
What do you think?
Do I want to take that chance?

I got too much to lose.
Before, you know, when we were just single together,
I had nothing to lose.
I have a little boy up there.
And if I ever caught Mark hurting me
or that little boy again,
I don't wanna be up for manslaughter.

Danny means more to me than Mark does.
Only because of what Mark does to me.
He just . . .
He doesn't realize it maybe, but he uh
squelches me.

God, I'm scared.
I don't wanna be alone for the rest of my life
with two kids.
And I can't rob my children of what little father they could
have.

STILL LIFE
Emily Mann

Set in 1978 and based upon actual interviews, *Still Life* examines three people who have, in one way or another, been deeply affected by the Vietnam War.

Nadine, (40s), a longtime friend of Mark's and both a career woman and mother, talks about the confusing role in society that men are asked to play.

NADINE: When I was younger,
I'd see a man in uniform
and I'd think:
what a hunk.
Something would thrill in me.

Now we look at a man in uniform—
A Green Beret, a Marine—
and we're repulsed somehow.
They don't know who they are anymore.
What's a man? Where's the model?

All they had left was being Provider.
Now with the economics,
they're losing it all.
And the younger ones
are worried about
the bull-shit in their lives.

Oh, I'm worried about men.
They're not coming through.
How could I have ever gotten married?
They were programmed to fuck.
Now they have to make love.
And they can't do it.
It all comes down to

fucking versus loving.

We don't like them in the old way anymore.
And I don't think they like us, much,
Now that's a war, huh?

THE VOICES OF SILENCE

Joan Vail Thorne

In this moving play, set in a dungeon in 1431, Joan of Arc is being held prisoner when she is visited by the Duchess of Bedford, cousin to the King. The Duchess, in pity, has come to offer her an escape from being burned at the stake. Joan refuses, believing it is her destiny to be a martyr.

In this opening scene, Joan, having been subjected to a humiliating and painful test for virginity the day before, is begging her voices to speak to her once more.

(*The dungeon cell of a medieval castle. What little light there is seeps in through a narrow slit opening high above the floor. There is a straw mat in the middle of the space, and a wooden pail off to one side. Dawn is breaking outside, and the vaguest glow allows us to see what could be the body of a girl, dressed in black tunic and tights, blindfolded, with foot chains, lying on the mat. There is a barely audible whimper, and then more silence—the pure stone-hard silence—before churchbells begin to ring. They are distant bells, definitely not in the immediate vicinity, probably from a distant village church calling the farmers' wives to early morning Mass. The body on the mat stirs, and struggles to sit up, with another stifled whimper. It is a girl, and she strains to hear something. After a moment or two she murmurs.*)*

JOAN: Please… Michael, St. Michael… Please

(*The churchbells seem to swell. A little more light enters throught the slit, and reveals more of the girl, her legs chained together at the ankles and her eyes blindfolded with a black cloth. She continues to listen desperately.*)

JOAN:: Sweet St. Catherine… Speak to me again in our blessed churchbells… (*She waits as the churchbells continue to ring.*)St. Margaret…? Speak to me, my blesséd saints! (*She waits for their answer before going on.*) What have I done? Why haven't I heard you since I was captured at Compiègne? (*Waiting again.*) You let God leave me in this hell-hole when

I've only done what you commanded me!

(*Suddenly the bells stop.*)

JOAN: No! Don't leave me in this silence! Please! I've done nothing to offend you, have I?... Have I? Ever since my victory at Orleans, I've... (*She stops abruptly.*) Is that it? "My" victory! "My?" I know it's not "my" victory. It's yours! I'm just the shepherd girl you used to fool the stupid English! I know my place. You made me what I am! You are my life!

(*A rooster begins to crow, and the light through the slit brightens the space a bit.*)

JOAN: (*Wooing him*) St. Michael, remember when you first came to me in the fields of Domrèmy—on the clouds my grandmère called God's pillows, full of poppies the color of Christ's blood? You wooed me away from my family, made my father curse me, and call me whore... Are you angered at me now because I fought for Paris on a feast day? Battles don't stop for benedictions! I had to fight! I can't wait for my voices to tell me every move!

(*Another set of less-distant bells begin to ring, and JOAN's heart leaps. But after a time she accepts the fact that she'll not hear her voices this time either.*)

JOAN: Nothing? Again and again? Only empty hollow bells forever?... Almighty God, why have you let them abandon me? I did your will, and you handed me over to mine enemy.

Men's Monologues

AFTER THE REVOLUTION
Nadja Tesich

After the Revolution is a drama about one family and America, in a hospital. As Michael lies unconscious, hit by a car, muttering about distant planets, various members of his family confront each other and their own dreams, lies, betrayals. They urge him to wake up.

Fred, 45, sits alone in his son's room and talks about his love and loneliness.

FRED: We rented a house on the beach that summer. I thought it would do everyone a lot of good, and Rachel had always liked the sea. You (*To MICHAEL.*) liked it too, do you remember? The waves would run after you and you would scream and run toward me. I have a picture of you like that. It's in my office and people usually ask me "who's that cute kid?"

We were as always, Rachel and I. She never became the young girl I knew, she didn't grow old either. Just absent, sort of, but only with me. She hugged and kissed the kids and fretted over them; they even had their own language, it seems. (*Pauses.*) No room for me. . . . Sometimes, I would hear laughter from the kitchen and run over, ready for something funny, but they would become silent as soon as I stepped in. At least she did.

(*Outside the window in the hall, two nurses whisper to each other.*)

Robert came to visit us with Angela, his latest. She was from California somewhere, a blond girl with long hair. We had a big dinner and a lot of wine and Rachel laughed and laughed the way kids do. She and Robert always told the same stories about their immigrant grandparents, what happened to them in America, how they got stuck in the elevators, or how they fought with each other and broke all the dishes, and how her grandfather slept in the hall in his fits of anger.

I never quite understood what was so funny, looking at them from here they seemed rather sad. At least to me. Peace and quiet, children and family is what I like.

It got quite dark, and a warm wind was blowing in from the ocean. We kept on drinking and laughing, and Robert put on a record. It was Latin, a kind of samba I think, something our parents liked. I don't know where he got it, you don't hear that kind of music any more. Robert and Angela started dancing and laughing; Robert could barely move. Rachel got up slowly, her eyes fixed somewhere else and started dancing too. I had never seen anyone move like that before. It was a dance of the whole body, swaying, happy, her face in a trance. Oh God, how happy she looked, and young too . . . Robert, drunk out of his mind, clapping, 'Go, baby, go' and then the record stopped. Rachel stood there, tears running down her cheeks...

I figured she was drunk and took her to bed. That living person of a few moments before was gone. Just gone, away from me. Making love to her wasn't different than always. Yet she had kindled a hope in me. She was there, lovely, living, but not for me. Some day, maybe...

I never said anything to her about all this, her loveliness and my despair . . . because I didn't know how . . . and was afraid of making things worse. Words once pronounced legalize the situation in a way that silence never does. I had always believed in wordless miracles, a funny thing for a doctor to say. . . . As I came downstairs the following morning, I heard them talking in the kitchen—young lovers, with Robert explaining his sister to Angela, very proud and almost bragging: (*He mimics.*)

"She was so much in love, you know."

And the other: "With whom?"

And Robert: "He was a jazz player, a black guy, quite handsome. It was some scandal back home."

And she: "Wow, I never expected anything like that from her. She seems so married."

"Oh, you're wrong," he all admiration. "She's some woman, my sister. You should have known her before."

And then in whispers, "Why did she marry him?" (That's me.)

"Beats me," he says. "to forget, maybe."

"Does he know?"

"She must have told him, I guess."

Well, now I knew, some of it at least, although I swear she liked me enough in the beginning. Nothing out of this world, just calm and sweet it was. She said I was kind and gentle. She even called me her big bear.

Well (*Mockingly, bitter.*), she was recovering from past blows and who to pick but a physician. It makes sense. (*He laughs.*)

Still, (*To* MICHAEL.) one thing is certain: I loved her then as I do now. I betrayed no one. (*Pause.*)

After that day, I stayed away from her for a while, still waiting, hoping. We went swimming and eating and took walks. I fished with Michael.

On that afternoon, Rachel and Robert were on the beach. With my field glasses I could see them laughing and splashing in the water. The kids were asleep upstairs. I said to myself, "Shall I sleep or swim?" and stood there making up my mind, when Angela came in out of somewhere in a thin yellow dress, smiling a big California smile at me and said, looking in my eyes, "What are you going to do this afternoon?" And I said (Why shouldn't I be as daring as the rest?) "Why, sit here with you."

How about that for a daring statement? Never been a real ladies' man you know. Never had any time for it, really. It was pre-med and med school and specialty and all that other stuff but then in all honesty I had no real inclinations either. I was born a family man, the kind that loves his wife and kids and simple uncomplicated things.

I don't remember how we got in the bedroom. Did I follow her or did she tell me to come in? Maybe it was all due to the humidity and the summer and my new daring. In any case, there we were and she was more than willing. She was nice to hold but it was not what I wanted. I knew it even then.

She left the next day. It was just as well. She might have expected more of the same and I was not going to provide it.

Afterwards, I thought that maybe she and Robert weren't really close, or that she was a bit nympho, or that he isn't such a hotshot lover as he pretends, or that something else was wrong. I kept wondering, but said nothing. How could I, being the guilty party?

We stayed there for the rest of the month. Rachel slept upstairs alone because of her back.

AFTER THE REVOLUTION
Nadja Tesich

After the Revolution is a drama about one family and America, in a hospital. As Michael lies unconscious, hit by a car, muttering about distant planets, various members of his family confront each other and their own dreams, lies, betrayals. They urge him to wake up.

Triggered by Michael's cries, (one, two, three, blast off, blast off) with Rachel nearby, Robert (35) remembers his youth, communal ecstasy on a street in New York. The entire cast supports him, the audience can join too.

ROBERT: Each time the cops charged I would almost shit in my pants. . . . Shh . . . keep it quiet. Nobody knows. Something in me ticked fast, like a bomb: this is it, this is it, this is it. It is coming, it is coming. . . . They came closer and closer, their helmets shining. On the outside, I must have looked quite determined and fearless. *I* was known for my courage.

(*Remembers.*) "You go there . . . you do this, you start moving,"

"Hell no, we won't go, go on everybody."

Yet, every time they charged, my stomach turned and turned, and I got dizzy.

"Hell, no, hell, no," "one, two, three, four, we don't want your fucking war, five, six, seven, eight, organize and smash the state." Smash, smash, smash...

"This is it, this is it, it," it ticked in me. In the last seconds, the fear would go away, totally go, just melt away. . . . The street was luminous, like in a dream. I was with others and they with me—and had I died then it would have been perfect. The problem was that even the cops and horses seemed somehow nice, a part of the total picture and I would lose my anger, a problem in a leader. Nobody knew it but me.

I should have died in those last seconds on the street with the cops and horses and friends and songs. . . . I would have been a hero, a martyr, the streets would have my name. Like the one in Hanoi. You remember the guy who burned himself in front of the U.N., around 1965. One of the first to go.

BREAKING THE PRAIRIE WOLF CODE
Lavonne Mueller

This play deals with the hardships a mother and daughter face on a wagon train heading West.

Bluster, one of the officers on the wagon train, chatters incessantly to Helen as he digs a grave for her dying fourteen-year-old daughter.

BLUSTER: Last good grave I dug was two days ago. Grandma Kittleson. Cholera. Wagon 12. (*Pause. To HELEN.*) Here good 'nough for you, Mrs. Yager?

(*HELEN doesn't answer and he takes her silence as a "Yes."*)

Oughta make the hole at least two miles from the train. For a good funeral, you need distance. So the procession kin spread out. (*BLUSTER stops digging to look at AMY and drinks.*)

I hear she aims ta see this grave herself? (*HELEN is silent. BLUSTER continues to dig.*)

(*To HELEN.*) I'm diggin' next ta bluegrass. Makes a nicer spot for a young girl like that. (*Pause.*) Yep . . . a grown woman's gonna take more space.

I take after my daddy . . . he had his tongue split to the middle. It worked both sideways and up and down. (*Pause. Stops digging.*)

Mam, you don't mind my saying . . . you'll have the time and all . . . oughta hand pick some of these rocks outta here. Don't make for a tidy grave. (*He goes back to digging.*)

I ever catch me a injun, I'll slit his tongue in half and take bets. Ta see if he's gonna be silent . . . or give his war yelps twice as much.

(*Stops digging. To HELEN.*) This here is a nice start for somethin' as little as her. (*Starts digging again.*) I had me a parrot to Land's End, Nevada. (*BLUSTER shovels dirt in HELEN's direction.*) I split-tongued that parrot . . . and that bird talked as fast with each half of its tongue as before—with the whole.

80

FOUR CORNERS
Gina Wendkos and Donna Bond

Four Corners explores the life of a woman who is an acute agoraphobic, someone who is terrified to leave her house, and the resulting emotional distress on her teenage son, Jimmy, and husband, Ralph.

Jimmy expresses both rage and pain in trying to cope with his mother's illness.

JIMMY: Shoot the bitch, that's right, I say *SHOOT THE BITCH!* . . . OR, (*Beat.*) . . . DROWN HER, ELECTROCUTE, POISON HER. . . . (*Begins to turn around, then faces back.*) . . . OH, WHAT THE FUCK, JUST GET IT OVER WITH. . . . *SHOOT THE UGLY COW BITCH!* (*Beat.*) . . . . WHAT? You think *I'M* a creep, *NO WAY, JOSE!* . . . Yeah, she's my mother, but, *SO FUCKIN' WHAT!* (*Pause.*)

DO I LOVE HER? Yeah, I love her.

DO I WANNA HELP HER? Yeah, I wanna help her . . .

DO I HOPE SHE GETS BETTER? Yeah, sure I do. (*Beat.*)

BUT, DO I WANNA SHOOT THE COW? (*He looks down for a second and then looks back up at audience*.)

DEFINITELY! (*Adds softly.*) . . . without a doubt. (*Beat.*)

Y'know like she just sits there, hardly moves. . . . I mean she goes to the bathroom and the kitchen and stuff like that, but; most of the time, she sits right there . . . (*Points to ANNA's back in living room.*) . . . playing cards and watching TV. So, I play this game with her sometimes, y'know just for fun...like she was furniture or something...Y'know 'cause she sits there all the time . . .

(*He sings it like a rhyme.*)

"OH, WHO DO I LIKE MORE? THE COUCH, THE STOOL, THE MOTHER, OR THE RUG? OH WHO DO I LIKE MORE, THE COUCH, THE STOOL, THE MOTHER OR THE RUG?" . . . and then I'll usually say, "Sorry, Mom . . . it's a toss up between the chair and the rug. Better luck tomorrow, O.K.?" (*JIMMY giggles.*)

. . . On a good day she laughs, and on a bad day . . . who remembers. (*Looks defensively at audience.*)

Why are you looking at me that way, Huh? You think I'm an ingrate? *NO WAY, MAN!* . . .

If she had cancer, I'd shave my head . . .

If she had polio, I'd limp for her . . .

If she had emphysema, I'd cough too . . . But, *AGORAPHOBIA!* . . . DREAM THE FUCK ON! . . . Sympathy from *ME!* . . . for her sitting in a room for 12 years and trembling. . . . *YEAH, 12 FUCKIN' YEARS* . . . of sitting there shaking, and getting on my nerves while me and him, (*Points at father on phone.*) has to get her everything from kotex to nail polish. . . . Later for that *SHIT!* (*Beat.*) which brings me back to . . . *SHOOT THE BITCH!*

(*JIMMY is ready to leave then changs his mind.*)

OH, and you wanna know what she says to me? (*Sarcastically.*) "Jimmy, I'm not afraid to *BE* outside, I'm afraid to *GO* outside." And I'm the asshole who lives with her.

FOUR CORNERS
Gina Wendkos and Donna Bond

Four Corners explores the life of a woman who is an acute agoraphobic, someone who is terrified to leave her house, and the resulting emotional distress on her teenage son, Jimmy, and husband, Ralph.

Ralph enviously reveals one of his co-worker's love-life.

RALPH: Y'know honey, Fred at work? Yeah. . . . Fred, you know, *you* know, I've told you about Fred. Fred and Madge? (*Sarcastic.*) Fred and Madge. Always showing off. Hah! But you know me, honey, I'm not impressed. Oh, you should hear him. You'd think he was the first man to have a dick. Oh, he really deserves a punch. And I'm the guy who should give it to him, too. Yeah, *me.* Why not? Huh? Why not? We sit there eight hours a day, and, yeah, even *lunch!* Eight hours every damned day he sits there with his stupid legs open like some stud or something, talking, talking, talking, bragging, bragging, bragging, Madge *this!* Madge *that!* And when she comes to pick him up you'd think she was Grace Kelly the way all these baboons whine and moan around her. Ooooh! And all the commotion when she sits. She does it on purpose. Her skirt, I mean. It rises just this far, and it's as if no one ever saw a goddamned kneecap before. I tell you Anna, to see grown men reduced to whimpering nitwits because of some young tart flaunting her privates, well, it's no wonder that I *choose,* that's right, that's what I tell 'em, I *choose,* out of my *choice,* y'hear, not to go with 'em to games and stuff, 'cause it's always Fred Fred Fred, talking, talking, talking, about Madge, Madge, Madge!

About her hair, *big deal!*

About her smile, *big deal!*

About her breasts! Yes! He talks about her breasts, in front of us! "Ooooh, they are sooo round! Each one a drop of honey!" Anna, he *does.* I wouldn't make up such filth. And those *mutts,* tongues hanging out like she was the first bitch on the block. It disgusts me. He tells me, *aaccchhh!* He tells me, well, *us,* he tells *us,* about where they do it. Where they *do* it! (*Incredulous horror.*) *Where they do it!* In the kitchen! In the den! In the garden! On the goddamned ironing board with her legs wide open . . . aaccchhh! It's disgusting! (*Sweetly.*) Anna, cupcake, do you know how lucky we are not to be like that . . . like . . . *animals.* Just like a bunch of wild mutts. I'm telling you, a bunch of mutts.

FOUR CORNERS
Gina Wendkos and Donna Bond

Four Corners explores the life of a woman who is an acute agoraphobic, someone who is terrified to leave her house, and the resulting emotional distress on her teenage son, Jimmy, and husband, Ralph.

Jimmy, addressing the audience, confides that he is afraid of becoming like his mother.

JIMMY: Look, you know how dogs begin to look like their owners? Do you think that could happen to me? I mean with Mom? I don't mean *look* like her, I mean I could start *thinking* like her. I'm normal. I *am*. Like you. But, the older I get, the more I get it. Not *get* it get it, but sorta get it. Y'know, like I understand how it could happen. Not totally, but, well, I get it. It's creepy, comin' home and knowin' that she's always gonna be sittin' *right there*. She's like a zombie or a ghost or somethin' . . . somethin' creepy, and I'm afraid I'm gonna turn into her, y'know like just talk myself into it, 'cause I keep thinkin' about it. I can't stop thinkin' about it. Do you think? Couldn't I turn into her?

MAGGIE AND MISHA
Gail Sheehy

Margaret Thatcher, ex-Prime Minister of Great Britain, has a momentous meeting with then-Soviet Premier Gorbachev. Gradually, as they cut through politics and policy, they connect on a human level.

Misha reveals a painful memory about his birthmark that influenced who he became.

GORBACHEV: "Misha, you are marked," they said, the village boys. "It's a curse. Maybe a curse on our village." One day the boys caught me. "You're—the devil!" they shouted. "Your curse must be washed away." They hung me off the bridge, head first, into the river.

[**THATCHER:** Oh, how dreadful!]

GORBACHEV: The water rushed into my throat, my lungs, but something made my head light—so light it floated like a cork on the river. I survived. But the mark, it was even bigger. Then they shouted, "For *sure* the devil is in Misha."

[**THATCHER:** How could they be so stupid?]

GORBACHEV: Russian peasants are very superstitious. I told my teachers I will become a diplomat. They said, "No, Mikhail Sergeyovich, you are the same as every other student." I said, "No, I wear a cossack hat. I *choose* to be different." So the village boys tied me to a horse, dragged my head through the dirt. But something made my head bounce. I survived. Mark was still there. Bigger. Darker. Strange, every time I did something different, it grew more. Maybe I am from a different strain. An aberration. Do you understand me?

[**THATCHER:** Utterly.]

GORBACHEV: Finally I knew it—this mark is not to hide forever—*this mark is my blind faith.* And you see today, every time I do something bold in the world, the taunts grow louder, but *my mark is bigger.*

NIEDECKER
Kristine Thatcher

Niedecker presents the touching story of poet Lorine Niedecker, her friend, her husband, and the young woman who loves and admires her.

Al, "a rough outdoorsman" and the spiritual opposite of the quiet, gentle Lorine, describes the joys of fishing.

Al: Any kind. Don't matter. But—if you're looking for real adventure there's nothing like going to get yourself a northern, nothing like it.

[**Lorine:** I've heard they're real fighters.]

Al: They're maniacs! Best bait in the world is frog—you slip the hook in his back, see, just under the spine, so he can swim free once he's in the water. When you've got him secure—and if you don't have much experience, it's a messy job, you've got to learn to do it clean—you cast that devil out as far as you can. Set your brake. Then, if you put the butt end of the rod in a piece of pipe on the shore and slip a tin can over the top of it, you're free to go about building a fire, taking a snooze, whatever you want; until you hear that can pop off the top of that pole. When you hear it go clattering, it's time to grab up the rod as fast as you can. The first order of business is setting the hook, and that's just a question of feel, learning when the fish is going for the heart of the frog. With a well-timed snap of the wrist, you can guarantee that fish a place on your supper table. But a northern pike is a fighter, a mean son of a bitch, who runs deep. You've got to play him just right or he'll snap your line. It's a matter of pulling back, reeling in, and easing off when you have to. At the very last, he'll come head first out of the water fighting mad, not like a trout or salmon, who ride their tails. It's the mouth that scares you.

[**Lorine:** Why?]

Al: Because a pike has a long snout and a top and bottom row of jagged teeth. Just when you think you can net him, he'll run at you again, so it looks like a damned alligator lunging up the line. Strikes terror into the heart.

STILL LIFE
Emily Mann

Set in 1978 and based upon actual interviews, *Still Life* examines three people who have, in one way or another, been deeply affected by the Vietnam War.

Mark, an ex-Marine and Vietnam vet in his thirties, describes the process that made him into a killer.

MARK: I don't think you understand.

Sure, I was pissed off at myself that I let myself go.
Deep down inside I knew I could have stopped it.
I could have just said:
I won't do it.
Go back in the rear, just not go out,
let them put me in jail.
I could have said:
"I got a tooth-ache," gotten out of it.
They couldn't have forced me.
But it was this duty thing.
It was like:
YOU'RE UNDER ORDERS.
You have your orders, you have your job,
you've got to DO it.

Well, it was like crazy.
At night, you could do anything . . .
It was free fire zones. It was dark. Then
All of a sudden, everything would just burn loose.
It was beautiful . . .
You were given all this power to work outside the law.
We all dug it.

But I don't make any excuses for it.

I may even be trying to do that now.
I could have got out.
Everybody could've.
If EVERYBODY had said *no,*
it couldn't have happened.
There were times we'd say:
let's pack up and go, let's quit.
But jokingly.
We knew we were there.
But I think I knew then
we could have got out of it.

See, there was a point, definitely,
when I was genuinely interested in trying to win the war.
It was my own area.
I wanted to do the best I could.
I mean I could have played it really low-key.
I could have avoided things,
I could have made sure we didn't move where we could have
   contacts.

And I watched the younger guys.
Maybe for six weeks there was nothing.
I'd drift in space wondering what he'd do under fire.
It only takes once.
That's all it takes . . .
and then—you dig it.

It's shooting fireworks off, the fourth of July.

STILL LIFE
Emily Mann

Set in 1978 and based upon actual interviews, *Still Life* examines three
people who have, in one way or another, been deeply affected by the
Vietnam War.

Here, Mark at last reveals some of the horror and pain he both suffered and
inflicted, in Vietnam.

MARK: I . . . I killed three children, a mother and father in cold
  blood. (*Crying.*)
[CHERYL: Don't.]
MARK: I killed three children, a mother and father. . . . (*Long
  pause.*)
[NADINE: Mark.]
MARK: I killed them with a pistol in front of a lot of people.

I demanded something from the parents and then
  systematically destroyed them.
And that's . . .
that's the heaviest part of what I'm carrying around.
You know about it now, a few other people know about it,
my wife knows about it,
and nobody else knows about it.
For the rest of my life . . .

I have a son . . .
He's going to die for what I've done.
This is what I'm carrying around.
That's what this logic is about with my children.

A friend hit a booby-trap.
And these people knew about it.
I knew they knew.
I knew that they were working with the VC infra-structure.

90

I demanded that they tell me.
They wouldn't say anything.
I just wanted them to confess before I killed them.
And they wouldn't .
So I killed their children
and then I killed them.

I was angry.
I was angry with all the power I had.
I couldn't beat them.
They beat me. (*Crying.*)

I lost friends in my unit. . . .
I did wrong.
People in the unit watched me kill them.
Some of them tried to stop me.

I don't know.
I can't. . . . Oh, God. . . .

A certain amount of stink went all the way back to the rear.
I almost got into a certain amount of trouble.

It was all rationalized,
that there was a logic behind it.
But they knew.
And everybody who knew had a part in it.
There was enough evidence,
but it wasn't a very good image to put out in terms of . . .
the Marine's overseas,

I have a child...
a child who passed through the age
that the little child was.
My son . . . my son
wouldn't know the difference between a VC and a Marine.

The children were so little.

I suppose I could find a rationalization.

All that a person can do is try and find words
to try and excuse me,
but I know it's the same damn thing
as lining Jews up.
It's no different
than what the Nazis did.
It's the same thing.

I know that I'm not alone.
I know that other people did it, too.
More people went through more hell than I did . . .
but they didn't do this.

I don't know . . .
I don't know . . .
if it's a terrible flaw of *mine*,
then I guess deep down I'm just everything that's bad.

I guess there's a rationale that says
anyone who wants to live that bad and gets in that
situation. . . .
(*Long pause.*)
but I should have done better.
I mean, I really strove to be good.
I had a whole set of values.
I had 'em and I didn't.
I don't know.

I want to come to the point
where I tell myself that I've punished myself enough.
In spite of it all,
I don't want to punish myself anymore,
I knew I would want to censor myself for you.
I didn't want you to say:
what kind of a nut, what kind of a bad person is he?
And yet, it's all right.
I'm not gonna lie.

My wife tries to censor me . . .
from people, from certain things.
I can't watch war shows.
I can't drive.
Certain things I can't deal with.
She has to deal with the situation,
us sitting around, a car backfires,
and I hit the deck.

She knows about the graveyards, and RJ and the woman.
She lives with all this still hanging.
I'm shell-shocked.

TALES OF THE LOST FORMICANS
Constance Congdon

Tales of the Lost Formicans concerns an assorted group of interrelated characters in a Colorado suburb being observed by what seems to be aliens from another planet.

Jerry, an offbeat neighbor in his thirties, believes that the moon landing was faked by the government.

JERRY: First off, they get a warehouse—doesn't have to be all that big—say, about the size of a Safeway. And the first thing they do is spray the walls and the ceiling flat black. And then they bring in about thirty loads of number ten gravel and they cover the floor with it. And then a couple, three loads of retaining wall rock—you know the size I mean—about as big as my fist, And they sprinkle that over this base of gravel. Now you know they've made some mounds here and there, so the floor isn't completely flat. They hang some lights from the girders and set up some big spots and they got a control booth in a corner. Then they bring in the machines—the lunar lander and the L E M. And that's when they set up the cameras, shout "Action!" and make a movie. Then they print it in black and white on crummy film in slow motion and pipe it onto all the television sets. And whammo—all the world sees a man land on the moon and plant the American flag. I mean, "Moon Rocks"?? Really. And don't talk to me about Voyager. They got a ride at Walt Disney World better than that. Think about it.

Permission Acknowledgments

MILK OF PARADISE by Sallie Bingham. Copyright © 1980, by Sallie Bingham. Reprinted by permission of the author and the Watkins/Loomis Agency. For more information, contact Watkins/Loomis Agency, 133 E. 35th St., New York, NY 10016.

MILLIE by Susan J. Kander. Copyright © 1986, by Susan J. Kander. Reprinted by permission of the author. For more information, contact Susan J. Kander, 133 W. 82nd Street, New York, NY 10024.

NIEDECKER by Kristine Thatcher. Copyright © 1985, by Kristine Thatcher. Reprinted by permission of the author. For more information, contact Kristine Thatcher, 6722 N. Bosworth, Chicago, IL 60626.

PARALLAX (IN HONOR OF DAISY BATES) by Denise Hamilton. Copyright © 1986, by Denise Hamilton. Reprinted by permission of the author. For more information, contact Denise Hamilton, 5301 Corteen Place, #9, N. Hollywood, CA 91607-2569.

PERSONALITY by Gina Wendkos and Ellen Ratner. Copyright © 1987, by Gina Wendkos. Reprinted by permission of the author. For more information, contact Gina Wendkos, 6431 LoPunto Drive, Los Angeles, CA 90068.

RELATIVITY by Marlane G. Meyer. Copyright © 1986, by Marlane Meyer. Reprinted by permission of the author's agent. For more information contact Peregrine Whittlesey, 345 East 80th Street, New York, NY 10021.

SCENE OF SHIPWRECK by Pamela Mills. Copyright © 1991, by Pamela Mills. Reprinted by permission of the author. For more information, contact Pamela Mills, 16 Portsmouth St., Cambridge, MA 02141.

STILL LIFE by Emily Mann. Copyright © 1982, by Emily Mann. Reprinted by permission of the William Morris Agency, Inc. on behalf of the Author. All rights reserved. CAUTION: Professionals and amateurs are hereby warned that STILL LIFE by Emily Mann is subject to a royalty. It is fully protected under the copyright laws of the United States of America, and of all countries covered by the International Copyright Union (including the Dominion of Canada and the rest of the British Commonwealth), and of all countries covered by the Pan-American Copyright Convention and